D0682400

The British Horse Society
Charity No. 210504

The BHS book of the
NATURAL HORSE

SARAH WIDDICOMBE

David and Charles

A DAVID & CHARLES BOOK
Copyright © David & Charles Limited 2008

David & Charles is an F+W Publications Inc. company
4700 East Galbraith Road
Cincinnati, OH 45236

953,221 | 636·1

Text copyright © Sarah Widdicombe 2008

Photographs by Matthew Roberts copyright © David & Charles 2008 except those listed below

Pages 6–7, 20, 24, 36, 37, 39, 49, 50 (lower left), 54 (left), 58, 61, 62, 63, 66 (top), 69 (right),
70, 80 (lower left), 85 (lower right), 166 (top left and right) 180, and 181 copyright © Horsepix 2008,
Sally and David Waters. With its roots in horse country and staffed by horse people, Horsepix is a leading provider
of high quality equestrian photography.

Pages 17,19, 30 (left), 68 (lower) and 67 copyright © 2008 Simon Palmer
Pages 34, 40–41 and 182 copyright © 2008 Sarah Widdicombe
Pages 42–43 copyright © 2008 Pixtal/PunchStock
Pages 68, 69 and 85 (top right) copyright © 2008 Jane Trollope
Pages 80 (top right) and 165 (lower left) copyright © 2008 Jenny Rolfe
Page 89 (top right) copyright © 2008 Eric Jones Photography
Page 158 and 159 copyright © 2008 Dianne Banks
Page 182 copyright © 2008 Lucy Mathews Photography

Illustrations on pages 21 and 23 by Maggie Raynor copyright © David & Charles 2008

ISBN-13: 978-0-7153-2496-7 hardback
ISBN-10: 0-7153-2496-9 hardback

Printed in China by Shenzhen RR Donnelley Printing Co. Ltd
for David & Charles
Brunel House   Newton Abbot   Devon

Commissioning Editor Jane Trollope
Assistant Editor Emily Rae
Designer Jodie Lystor
Production Controller Beverley Richardson
Photographer Matthew Roberts

WESTMEATH COUNTY LIBRARY

Visit our website at www.davidandcharles.co.uk

David & Charles books are available from all good bookshops;
alternatively you can contact our Orderline on 0870 9908222 or write
to us at FREEPOST EX2 110, D&C Direct, Newton Abbot, TQ12 4ZZ
(no stamp required UK only); US customers call 800-289-0963
and Canadian customers call 800-840-5220.

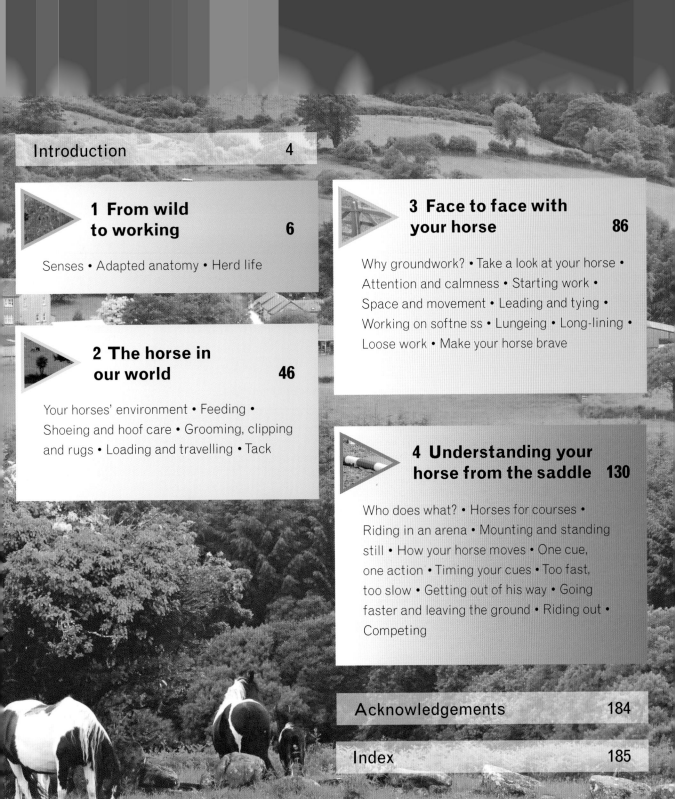

INTRODUCTION

This book is a simple, sympathetic look at how horses react to and deal with the human world, and how best to manage their natural reactions to life, both good and bad. It explores the 'natural' horse, explaining why he is designed as he is, and how this affects how he perceives, understands and performs what we ask of him.

Chapter one takes a look at the physical and behavioural nature of the horse, how he is perfectly built to survive in the environment from which he evolved. Chapter two offers suggestions for making an average daily regime easier for the horse, within the inevitable restrictions that modern life imposes on us all. Chapter three is a practical guide to really effective handling and groundwork, and the final chapter looks at ways to communicate with the horse from the saddle that make it easy for him to comply with our requests. Throughout the book there is practical advice on introducing new experiences and overcoming existing problems in a non-confrontational but effective way.

The BHS Book of the Natural Horse invites us to set a higher standard for ourselves and for our horses. It shows how the horse's nature is to seek an easy path by doing the right thing, and that it is usually ineffective communication and inconsistency that lead to problems and unwanted behaviour. We don't have to accept a horse that mows us down, can't be ridden away from his stable mates, or spooks at everything. We just need to get better at showing the horse what we want and being consistent in our requests, by stepping up into the role required of us by the successful horse-human relationship, with all the responsibility that that entails.

You may already have a great partnership with your horse, but if you take on board even some of the information contained in this book your horse will really appreciate the difference, and you will reap the rewards too.

1 FROM WILD TO WORKING

The single most important point we need to understand about the horse is that he is a prey animal. His number one priority is survival, and his primary means of escape from predators is to run. Everything about the horse – his physique, his behaviours, his natural lifestyle – is geared to this end, and has profound consequences for his reactions when we bring him into our human world and ask him to work with us.

This chapter looks at the horse as he is: the instinctive animal that still lives within every domestic equine, however far removed his life may now be from that of his wild ancestors. Only when we understand this can we begin to devise ways of keeping, training and riding horses that will keep them comfortable, content and happy to co-operate in everything we want to do together.

THE HORSE'S SENSES

Understanding how the horse receives information from his environment and uses his senses is the first step towards gaining a 'horse's-eye' view of the world, which in many ways is quite different to our own. His senses feed him information that his lightning-quick reflexes allow him to act upon instantly if needed, ensuring his safety from predators.

Vision

The horse's large and expressive eyes are often regarded as one of his most beautiful features, but they are not just pretty appendages – the way the eyes function is essential to the horse's survival.

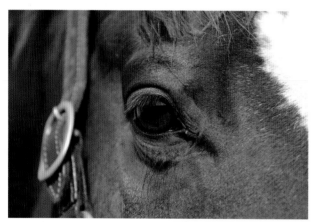

△ **The horse's eye mirrors his emotions, from heavy lidded and relaxed...**

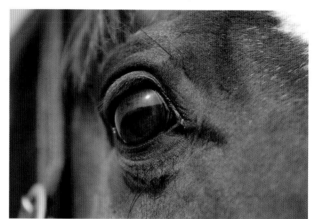

△ **...to wide open and fixed intently on an object that has caught his attention.**

△▷ **In this theoretical demonstration, the horse is looking directly ahead at the parked cars. Wrap the outside edges of the pages towards each other to get an idea of how the horse see this yard and buildings. He also has everything else in this panorama in view, including his own flanks.**

Field of vision

It is small wonder that the horse's eyes are so attractive – they are the largest in relation to body size of any land mammal. They are set wide apart on either side of the head, which gives the horse almost 360-degree vision. This is an important advantage for a prey animal. It also means he may see things behind him that a rider or handler does not and react to them – how many times have you heard riders report that their horse suddenly shot forward 'for no reason'?

◁ **Because his eyes are positioned on the sides of his head, in order to focus directly in front of him the horse has to swivel his eyes forward, exposing the whites.**

The horse has a blind spot of approximately three degrees directly behind him, over his back and extending out past his hindquarters. This feature of ther horse's visual field has implications for both working him from the ground and getting him used to carrying a rider. When using long lines or loose schooling, many horses become worried when the handler disappears as they step directly behind, so it is important to get your youngster used to 'changing eyes' as you cross from one side to the other. If you don't, you may be in for a surprise the first time you get on him from the left side and he suddenly catches sight of you above him on his right!

There is also a blind spot directly in front of the horse that extends for a metre or so. You therefore need to remember that he cannot see your hand moving up to pet him on the front of his face. A horse that allows you into his blind spot is showing a lot of trust.

To each side of the horse is a large area of monocular vision – he sees a different 'view' in each eye, and can move each eye independently. Again, this is an advantage to a prey animal that needs to keep checking what is going on all around him. There are differing opinions on whether the information a horse receives via one eye is transferred by his brain from one side to the other (see box 'Left and right' on page 10). If not, it is unsurprising that he reacts to an object he has seen only in one eye when it is presented to the other; in effect, he has never seen it before. On the other hand, the horse's reaction often appears less marked than when he initially saw the object with his first eye, implying that at least some information is transferred.

Directly in front, beyond his blind spot, the horse has an area of binocular vision covering about 65 degrees. Here, judging distance, depth and the speed of another animal or object is easier, although he may use other 'clues' such as perspective effects – the further away an object is, the smaller it appears – to judge these factors in his monocular areas. If this were not the case, the horse would have difficulty making essential judgements about his environment in everyday life, let alone performing some of the complex tasks we ask of him.

More recent research suggests the horse has a 'visual streak' – a narrow, horizontal band – on the retina of his eye, so that he moves his head and neck to allow light from objects he wants to see in detail to fall on this streak.

Left and right

One theory suggests that the horse prefers to have us (or any unfamiliar or threatening object) on his left, not because he has always been handled from that side or his body is slightly bent that way naturally, as some suggest, but because he instinctively likes to use the right side as an escape route and is uncomfortable if it is blocked.

This means that, if he can, the horse will tend to look at new objects with his left eye first, while the right eye checks the possibilities for escape. In a herd he will accept horses on both sides, so if he remains uncomfortable with a person on his right, this implies that the horse still sees humans as a threat.

This theory postulates that visual information *is* transferred from one side of the brain to the other, so it is not that the object seen on the left is not recognized when seen on the right, rather that the horse's *emotional response* differs between the two sides. Perhaps early horse handlers recognized this and began the horse's training from the left, giving rise to a convention that is now hard to break.

An alternative theory suggests that individual horses favour one eye or the other, much as we are either left or right handed. Whatever the truth, it is certainly the case that horses are not happy to look at scary objects, or us, with both eyes until they are sure that what they are seeing poses no immediate threat. We need to bear this in mind when setting up training situations, in order to keep the horse calm and ourselves safe.

1) This horse has approached the plastic sheet with some trepidation, his eyes and ears riveted upon it. As he gets up close, he decides that stepping onto the plastic would definitely be a step too far and stops dead. He lowers his head to investigate further and keep the obstacle in focus.

2) The handler asks the horse to step onto the plastic, and his right ear pointed in her direction shows he is paying attention to her request. But his courage has deserted him and, while he keeps his eyes on the 'blue monster' in case it makes any sudden moves, his left ear checks out his escape route and he moves away in that direction.

3) The horse's attention is distracted by a movement in the distance on which he focuses intently with both eyes and ears, blanking out the problem of the plastic sheet – the equine equivalent of burying your head in the sand.

4) The handler blocks the horse's escape to the left – and the same scenario is then played out to the right.

5) The horse has decided he has to face his demons, and lowers his head to check out the plastic up close with eyes, ears and nose.

6) He makes up his mind and walks across, head lowered to keep an eye on his footing and ears checking out his other options in case he needs to make a quick getaway.

Bringing it into focus

The horse cannot focus well on objects that are close to him. He may therefore back away from something that suddenly appears in front of him out of his blind spot – first, because he is startled and, second, to bring it into better focus. Our own eyes focus automatically, by adjusting the thickness of the lens. In contrast, to focus on an object the horse must move his head.

The horse can focus well on objects that are at a distance. This explains why your horse may suddenly stop and stare transfixed at something on the horizon that you can barely detect.

The length of the horse's face – which enables him to graze while still seeing above the grasses – means he cannot see the ground beneath his feet and has to rely on the image he had a few strides earlier. To see directly in front of him (say, to negotiate a stream), he needs to drop his head.

Special sensitivities

The horse's vision is specially adapted in several ways to perceive:
• the slightest movement – in case predators are around.
• quality of movement – jerky movement from humans mimics what other horses do when startled and may alarm him; hesitant movement will make him unsure too; very slow movements are characteristic of a stalking predator.
• changes in the appearance of the environment – these could be a clue that a predator is now lurking. Because of this awareness, your horse may react when you ride past an object that was not at the side of the road the day before or has been moved from its original position.

Spooking

A horse may spook:
• when something close by comes into focus as he moves away;
• when something comes into sharp focus as light from it hits his 'visual streak';
• if his head is restricted when ridden, so that he cannot turn it to focus on an object and therefore has to move his whole body.

1-3) As the horse approaches a jump, there comes a moment when the obstacle disappears from his field of vision and he has to 'remember' where to take off in order to negotiate it safely.

Light, dark and colour

Horses can distinguish colours, an ability that helps to prevent ambush by predators. However, ideas on exactly which colours they can see are updated regularly as further research is carried out. One issue most people agree on is that white can produce a strong reaction in horses.

The ability to see colour is not as important to the horse as the ability to detect movement (see page 11): a predator may change its coat colour with the seasons, for example, but it is always essential for the horse to know if a predator is on the move.

Horses have good night vision. If they did not, they would be easy pickings for predators once the sun went down. On the other hand, horses seem to have difficulty dealing with shadows and dark areas, especially where they are going to step, as these may indicate false ground and a horse cannot afford to get his feet trapped or be brought down. The horse's ability to adapt to changes in light levels is probably not as good as ours, as in an outdoor life such changes are generally more gradual than, say, moving from bright sunshine outside into the interior of a dark stable.

Processing the information

We now have a great deal of knowledge about how horses see the world around them, but we will never have a horse's brain. So, even if we know how his vision works, we cannot know what mental image his brain creates from that information. We can therefore never experience exactly what it is like to look at the world through the eyes of a horse.

△ The internal stable in this old barn presents a very dark picture to the horse as he is led inside on a bright, sunny day. A horse that is unfamiliar with the set-up might baulk when first asked to step into this loose box.

△ On leaving the stable, the situation is reversed: the horse has to step from relative darkness into bright sunlight and his eyes will need time to adjust.

Hearing

The horse's hearing is another essential component in his constant vigilance for predators. Whatever its size or the detail of its shape, which vary from breed to breed and from horse to horse, the equine ear has evolved to pick up the slightest sound that might signify danger.

What can he hear?

The horse cannot hear low-pitched sounds as well as we can, although he may detect them as vibrations; conversely, he can pick up much higher pitched sounds than we do. Remember this when your horse appears to react to something you cannot hear.

The horse's ears are very mobile and can rotate through almost 180 degrees, enabling them to collect sounds from all directions and pinpoint their source far more accurately than we can. Crucially, the ears can be moved independently, allowing the horse to focus on two places at once. This is a huge advantage to a prey animal, since not all predators hunt alone.

It is well known that horses are often more tense and anxious when the wind is blowing hard. This is because windy conditions not only move objects around but also distort sounds. The horse becomes more reactive as noises appear louder, can be picked up from farther away and may be difficult to identify. Horses hate uncertainty: they cannot feel safe until they know who or what is on the move around them and exactly where it is. This is why your horse may react more to a light rustle in the bushes whose source is not visible than to a noisy tractor working in an open field as you ride past.

◁ The horse's ears are extremely mobile. He can swivel them in opposite directions to pick up sounds from all around him...

◁ ...prick them forward to focus on something up ahead...

◁ ...and then keep one pointed forward while the other begins to swivel sideways again.

What the ears tell us

The position of a horse's ears indicates where his attention is focused and whether he is alert or relaxed. Learning to 'read' this accurately can be a great help in training and riding your horse (see pages 90–92 and 97).

• Ears pricked sharply forward indicate the horse is looking with binocular vision (see page 9) and is focused intently on some object that may be causing him excitement (such as another horse in the distance) or concern (such as washing flapping on a line). This is not generally desirable when you are riding, as your horse is definitely not focusing any part of his attention on *you*!

• Ears pointing in different directions mean the horse is focusing on two places at once. This can be an advantage when riding, as he can focus partly on you and what you want him to do next, and partly on the terrain you are crossing or what is up ahead.

• Both ears pointing back but not tightly pinned indicate the

When the position of this mare's ears is combined with the focus of her eyes, the position of her head and neck, and her alert demeanour, we get a much fuller picture of her state of mind and the focus of her attention than from the ears alone.

horse is listening to something behind him or is focusing intently on his rider. It can sometimes be a sign that he is anxious or confused about the way he is being ridden.

• Ears held in a relaxed but not floppy 'V' shape, occasionally flicking to give momentary attention to a specific sound or movement, mean the horse can focus without tension on his rider and, when necessary, on what is going on around him.

△ **The position of this horse's ears indicate that he is paying relaxed attention to his rider while checking out the photographer away to his right.**

△ **Going the other way, towards a corner of the school overhung by trees, his attention leaves his rider to focus on whatever dangers may be lurking there. His ears are pricked sharply forward and his eyes are focusing directly ahead. Tension shows in his raised head and braced neck.**

The ears and communication

The ears are also a means of communication and indicate a horse's mood. For example:

• Ears laid flat back are threatening to another horse or human, and may be backed up with a bite or kick if necessary to get his point across.

• Ears lightly pricked towards an unfamiliar object (and often accompanied by snorting) indicate the horse is curious but also somewhat wary. In a training or riding situation, take note of this and work to build the curiosity and reduce the fear (see pages 125–129).

• Ears flopped out to the sides mean the horse is extremely relaxed and happy in his situation – carry on grooming or massaging him, as he is thoroughly enjoying it!

Of course, we can also communicate back to the horse via his hearing, by teaching him to respond to particular sounds and/or words during training.

△ **The chestnut horse does not appreciate the grey's attentions and lays his ears flat back to get him to move away. Tension also shows in the tightness of his mouth and muzzle area.**

The skin and touch

When we look at a horse, what we usually notice first is the colour of his coat. Beneath this covering of hair lies his skin, which together with the coat protects all the underlying structures. To perform this function, the horse's skin is flexible but very strong, and is able to repair itself if damaged.

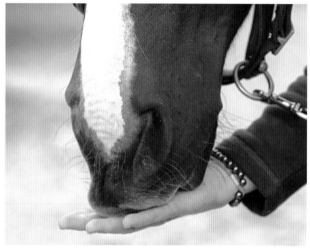

△ **A horse's muzzle is many times more sensitive than a human hand.**

The sensitive horse

The horse's skin is packed with nerve endings and is very sensitive to touch, especially in certain areas of the body such as the girth and stifle areas, behind the elbows and between the back legs.

It is well known that any horse is so sensitive he can feel a fly land on him; he can also shiver his skin to move that fly away. A horse that appears dull to the touch of your hands, or your legs when riding, may have a natural tendency to be less sensitive than average, but it is more likely that his sluggish responses have been largely made this way by poor handling and training. The same is true of one that appears over-sensitive and cannot tolerate the feel of human touch in certain areas of his body (see Chapters 3 and 4).

A horse's muzzle has more nerve endings per square centimetre than a human finger and is very mobile, which is very useful for sorting food. The whiskers here are very important for investigating by touch where the horse can't see, so should not be removed (see page 69). This is often an area where foals and unhandled older horses find it difficult to accept human touch because the whiskers are so sensitive. It is therefore not surprising that the horse may react (usually by throwing up his head and backing away) the first few times he feels your hand and a headcollar noseband passing up and down over his muzzle.

△ **A mare will touch and smell her foal frequently, especially in the early days, as an important means of identification and bonding.**

Touch and communication

Touch has important effects on horses. For example:

• Mares and foals touch each other frequently, reinforcing the bond between them. The foal also learns about the meaning of more forceful touch: his dam may nip his hindquarters if he accidentally bites while feeding from her, or she may push or bite him to get him to move where she wants him to go.

• Horses within a herd perform mutual grooming, cementing the bond of group membership (see page 40).

• Unfriendly or aggressive touch from either another horse or a human provokes resentment and sometimes an aggressive reaction in return.

• When riding, we use touch to communicate our requests to horses through our hands, legs and seat. The quality of this touch is important – on this depends the quality of the horse's response (see Chapters 3 and 4).

◁ **This horse is seeking out the tastiest plants to eat from the hedgerow, using her mobile muzzle to sort through the vegetation.**

Smell and taste

The senses of smell and taste are very important for providing information to the horse. Smells are particularly useful, as they tend to linger for a long time.

How horses use smell

Horses can smell a predator from approximately 200m (220yd) away on a still day, and as much as 1km (⅝ mile) with a favourable wind. This generally gives them a more than acceptable head start on any pursuer.

The mare in the foreground has just urinated where the stallion is now standing, and he is investigating her hormonal state through smell using the 'flehmen' posture.

In the herd

Within their own herd, horses use smell in a number of ways. Mares use it to identify their foals and reject those of other mares – this has obvious implications for foal fostering in domestication. A stallion identifies which of his mares is in oestrus (in 'season') and ready to be mated using smell. To do this, he curls back his upper lip in the 'flehmen' posture to trap the scent in his nostrils, where it is analysed by a special organ called the vomeronasal or Jacobsen's organ.

Horses will smell dung piles to identify other horses that have used the area. The various smells provide plenty of information about which horses have passed by, when and with whom. A stallion will dung, and sometimes urinate, on top of a rival's pile to replace the smell with his own. He sniffs the dung pile, steps over it, steps back if necessary to line up, dungs, and then turns around to sniff his own dung. Mares and (in domestication) most geldings sniff the pile but don't usually bother with the rest of the routine. They then dung outside the pile rather than on top of it (in a field, creating an ever-increasing latrine area). In feral horses, dung piles may help herds avoid each other, thereby eliminating the need for direct conflict.

Horses greet each other by exchanging breath, receiving information through smell including where the other horse has been and who he has been with. Herd members may do this when they have not seen or interacted with another herd member for a relatively short time; stallions check their mares regularly in this way. This is also the first act on meeting an unfamiliar horse: the exchange of breath tells a horse whether he knows the other or not. Herd membership is crucial to each horse's survival, and he needs to know who belongs and who is an outsider. Herd members often roll in one patch of mud, covering their own smell with that of the herd.

Other smells

Horses may become alarmed by some smells – anything from pigs to perfume – possibly because these scents are particularly strong and not part of the horse's everyday experience so may signify danger. We may not understand exactly why a particular horse reacts strongly to certain odours, but we need to be aware of this possibility when he suddenly behaves in an apparently inexplicable fashion.

△ **These horses live together, but even when they have been separated for only an hour or two for work they still check each other out through exchange of breath.**

More usefully, perhaps, it appears that horses may be able to locate water by smell from some distance away. In addition, the verdict is still open on whether horses find their way primarily by smell, as they tend to travel upwind.

How horses use taste

The horse selects food and water initially through smell, and he may refuse to eat or drink if this is not acceptable. This is a common experience with domestic horses if we try to give them wormers in feed, or provide tap water when they are used to a natural stream (and vice versa). If the smell is acceptable, the horse will then taste the food or water.

The horse may react to unfamiliar tastes by throwing his head up and down, often followed by flehmen. A mouthful of grasses that has been smelled and then sorted using his mobile muzzle may still contain some plants with an unfamiliar or unpleasant taste, and the horse will reject these as he continues to chew the rest of his mouthful. Domestic horses may also sort their concentrated food in this way until certain components whose smell and taste they do not like remain in an otherwise empty feed bowl.

This lengthy series of checking actions is important to the horse because he cannot afford to make mistakes with food or water and become ill – this is a death sentence for a prey animal.

ADAPTED ANATOMY

The horse's physique is superbly adapted to his lifestyle as a grazing prey animal that uses flight as his first line of defence – but it's not quite as well suited to living and working in the ways we ask him to. His senses (see pages 8–19) and extremely rapid reflexes prepare him for flight in an instant, while his body is designed for running fast, in more or less a straight line.

Evolution

The horse has evolved over 55 million years from a small, forest-dwelling browser with separate toes (the 'dawn horse', *Hyracotherium*) that ran and hid to avoid predators into a large, plains-living grazer with hooves (*Equus*) that flees to escape.

The ground-gripping toes and relatively flexible, arched spine of *Hyracotherium* allowed this creature to easily twist and turn at speed through his forest habitat – his movement would have been something between that of a cat and a dog. Around 40 million years ago open spaces began to appear in the forest, and these eventually developed into dry, sparsely covered grass-plains, prairies and savannah. However, it was not until around 22 million years ago that horses began to adapt to grazing and fleeing on this relatively level, firm terrain, where running in a straight line is the most efficient mode of flight.

△ These feral horses are living on the dry, plains-type terrain to which equine anatomy and physiology are ideally adapted.

As well as adaptations in the teeth, jaws and intestinal tract, to allow for chewing and digesting the fibrous grasses, changes also began to take place in the anatomy of the horse's spine. The arched shape started to straighten out, and stronger couplings developed between the front, middle and back sections of the horse's body: withers appeared, and the loins lost much of their lateral flexibility. All these developments resulted eventually in a relatively rigid spine adapted to straight-line flight.

It was at this time that changes also began to take place in both the overall size of the horse of this period (*Parahippus*) and the proportions of his body and limbs. If we compare our own limbs with those of the modern horse (*Equus caballus*), it is interesting to note that:

• the major bones are the same in both humans and horses;
• on average, the length of the upper arm (humerus) and thigh (femur) is the same in both;
• it is the huge elongation of the rest of the bones that gives the horse's limbs their much greater overall length (see page 23).

It is this increase in the overall size and length of the limbs that has conferred on the horse his ability to elude pursuers at great speed.

The modern horse is the product of millennia of adaptation to life as a prey animal on the wide-open plains, as evidenced by the anatomy of his various parts.

Head and neck

The bulk of the horse's head is made up of long nasal chambers, giving him a powerful sense of smell (see pages 18–19) and plenty of room for breathing efficiently while moving at speed.

The lower jaw and the muscles used for eating are extremely important for an animal that grazes almost continuously, and make up most of the remainder of the horse's head. The parts of the teeth we cannot see – because they are set into the jaws – are far longer than the parts we can see (see page 25). Consequently, there is no room for the horse's eye to be positioned directly over the line of the teeth in the upper jaw, and the head is therefore elongated so that the eye sits higher up in the skull. This confers the added advantage to the horse of being able to graze while at the same time keeping a lookout above the grasses for any hint of danger.

The long neck lowers the horse's head to the grass and is flexible, allowing him to move his head easily for vision, self-grooming and, very importantly, balance while in motion.

Spine

While the horse's neck is quite flexible, his spine is relatively rigid from the withers back. An adaptation for straight-line flight (see page 21), this also helps to minimize the degree of up-and-down leg motion, thereby conserving energy.

However, relatively rigid is not the same as absolutely rigid. A degree of lateral movement in the spine allows the horse to bend in order to groom his itchy spots (although much of this is achieved by bending the neck – the cervical

△ It is clear that as this mare reaches around to scratch her stifle area, most of the lateral bend is taking place in her neck (cervical spine). The mid-back (thoracic spine) – where the rider will sit – bends very little at all.

spine); it also allows the well-schooled horse to bend around circles and turns (see pages 116–117 and 149).

There is also some up-and-down movement in the spine, particularly in the lumbo-sacral joint that articulates the horse's hindquarters with the rest of his back. This facility allows for staling, for bucking to dislodge a predator and for coiling the hindquarters further underneath the horse's body to enable him to depart at speed from a standing start. This movement is also key to the horse being able to carry a rider comfortably, and one we utilize when riding a horse in collection (see pages 163–165).

1

2

3

4

5

1) This sequence of photographs gives an idea of the range of movement available in a horse's spine. Here the dun pony kicks out athletically at his younger fieldmate, who easily avoids contact by swinging his head and neck away.

2) The pony coils his hindquarters underneath him and executes an impressive sliding stop.

3) The grey collects himself, taking his weight on his hindquarters, rounding his back and neck, and lightening his forehand, ready to stop and spin off in the opposite direction.

4) Both horses lengthen their bodies as they set off fast down the field, then the pony coils his hind end again as he prepares to turn right while the grey stretches into a gallop.

5) The pony has his hindquarters lowered and legs well underneath him as he wheels away to the right. The grey lifts his back and brings his head down, creating a spectacular arch with his spine as he slows within a stride or two, ready to follow his friend.

Limbs and feet

As discussed on page 21, the horse's limbs have evolved by elongating the bones to provide maximum leverage and therefore speed for flight.

At the top of the forelimb, the shoulder blade (scapula) is not fixed in position by bone (as in humans) but by muscle and connective tissue alone. This means it can swing back and forth freely, allowing the legs to move faster and reach further to cover the ground more quickly.

The upper part of the limbs – from the knee upwards in the forelimb and hock up in the hindlimb – provides muscle power. It is close to the pivot point and does not have to move far, so can carry the extra weight of the muscles. The power is transmitted to the lower limbs via tendons that act much like springs, thereby increasing energy efficiency.

The lower part of the limbs is elongated to form a long lever, with no muscles so that it is light and the weight to be moved is minimized. The trade-off is that the lower limb is more vulnerable to injury as there is no muscular protection.

The overall effect of these anatomical arrangements is to increase speed *and* save energy. The horse has explosive speed – around 75kmph (47mph) – over about 500m (1/3 mile), allowing him to outpace *and* outdistance most predators.

The standing horse

Horses have a 'stay apparatus' that locks the hindlegs to reduce energy use when standing, as muscles are not involved in keeping the animal up. This enables the horse to rest standing up, which is safer for a prey animal than lying down, although horses will lie down – sometimes to sleep lying flat out for short periods – in safe circumstances.

Hooves

The feet of *Hyracotherium* were fairly similar to a dog's paws, with four toes on the front feet and three on the back (see page 20). From this beginning, the horse's foot developed over millions of years into the single digit we see today – the hoof.

The outer structures of the horse's hoof are strong and hard to protect against bruising and injury on the relatively dry, firm and sometimes rocky terrain of the plains and prairies where the horse evolved. Today's horses show some adaptations in hoof shape for harder or softer ground – smaller, more upright feet on desert breeds such as the Arab or the feral horses of Namibia; bigger, flatter feet with feathers on (often heavier) breeds that live on wetter land in parts of Europe and the UK. Overall,

however, the horse's hoof is still a product of, and best suited to, life on the type of dry, short-grass turf found on plains terrain. This provides some challenges for hoofcare in domestic horses living in wetter, lusher areas of the world (see pages 62–64).

Parts of the complex structure within the horse's hoof are flexible, to allow it to cope with the transfer of energy during movement – hoof to ground, ground to hoof and into the stride at lift-off. This is especially important when such a large animal is travelling at speed.

The wall of the hoof is ever-growing, thereby counteracting the wear it receives as the horse crosses the ground. Horses naturally travel many tens of kilometres each day (see page 31), so this feature is essential. Other structures in the hoof, including the frog, sole and bars, also grow and adapt according to the wear they receive and the environment in which the horse lives.

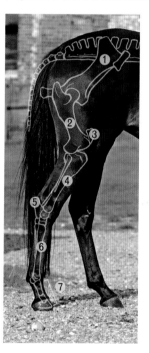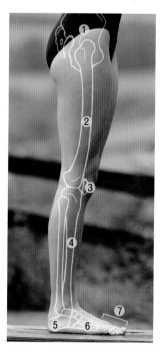

△▷ **Our arms and legs are comprised of the same bones as the horse's fore- and hindlegs. However, while the upper limb bones in the horse aren't that much different in length to a human's, the lower limb bones (which correspond to those in our hands and feet) are greatly elongated as an adaptation for hugely enhanced speed. The bones correspond as marked: 1 pelvis, 2 femur, 3 patella, 4 tibia, 5 calcaneus, 6 metatarsal/s and 7 phalanges. The horse is, in effect, standing on his middle fingertip/tiptoe.**

Heart and lungs

Although the horse spends much of his time grazing in a leisurely fashion or moving relatively slowly from place to place, his heart and lungs are both quite large. This is anatomy designed not for everyday life but for worst-case scenarios: the organs must be large enough to fuel the horse's muscles efficiently during bursts of movement at high speed when he needs to escape a predator.

▽ **One of the reasons we find horses so impressive is their explosive speed. In order to sustain this for long enough to outpace and outdistance a predator, the horse requires large, powerful heart and lungs.**

Eating and digestion

The process of eating and digestion begins with the horse seeking out palatable grasses and other plants. His lips are very mobile and are ideal for selecting and lining up food for the front line of teeth (incisors) to grab hold of (see page 16).

Teeth

The horse's incisors are well adapted for tearing off tough stalks and fibrous grasses; these are then passed to the back teeth (molars), which grind them up using a shearing action.

Between the front and back rows of teeth in each jaw there is a gap, called the bars. This is where the bit rests when a horse is ridden.

With such an abrasive diet – which from time to time also includes leaves, berries, bark and even mud – the horse's teeth are by necessity very strong. The part of the teeth that can be seen when the horse opens his mouth is small by comparison to that lodged in the gums and skull (see page 21). As the horse eats his fibrous diet, his teeth wear over time; they also grow out continuously from the jaws to compensate for this wear. Eventually, in old age, the horse will start to run out of tooth. In feral horses, it is failure of the teeth that most often spells the end.

Digestion and feeding pattern

The design of the horse's intestinal tract is specially adapted for digesting tough, fibrous, low-energy plants and grasses as found on plains terrain. In fact, the horse thrives on the poorest quality, lowest protein diet of any large herbivore.

Cattle and sheep have to rest between bouts of eating, regurgitating their food and chewing it again – this is known as rumination or 'chewing the cud'. In contrast, in horses the caecum – a fermentation chamber that breaks down plant cellulose – allows the animal to eat small amounts almost continuously, and therefore to run without ever having to carry a full stomach of food with him. This is a huge advantage when the horse needs to flee a predator at a moment's notice.

As the horse is able to eat almost continuously, for a total of around 16 hours per day (see page 31), he can survive on low-quality feed. This is because he pushes more food through his system in 24 hours and extracts more energy per unit of time than do cattle and sheep. From this continuous feeding, the horse has developed a psychological need to chew, in addition to the physiological need to process his food. Both of these aspects have important implications when we bring the horse into domestication (see pages 59–61).

At the other end of the process, the horse dungs many times per day as his food passes through his system. He can also defecate to order, so he is able to lighten his load at any time if he feels flight may shortly be necessary.

△ The horse tears off mouthfuls of grass using his incisor teeth.

△ The horse chews with the molar teeth at the back of the mouth, using a shearing action as the jaws move from side to side.

The brain, intelligence and thinking

There has always been debate about the nature of the horse's brain, how he thinks and what he can understand. At one extreme, the horse is classified as unintelligent or even 'stupid', his thought processes totally unlike those of a person. At the other, the horse thinks, feels and reacts much as humans do.

Today, most people agree that the truth lies somewhere in between (it's where exactly that 'somewhere' is that is still the subject of debate!). It then becomes a matter of understanding the similarities *and* the differences between the ways in which horses and humans think and behave.

Since we cannot have a verbal conversation with a horse, ideas about what and how he thinks must be deduced from his behaviour. The interpretations we place on this can vary: it is difficult enough for us to unravel the thoughts and feelings behind the behaviour of another person, let alone another species. However, there are some points we can safely make about the horse's brain and responses.

Priorities

As humans, we tend to call the ability to solve problems 'intelligence', but in his everyday life the feral horse doesn't need this so much. A good proportion of his brain power is related to moving and balancing his large body, sometimes at speed, rather than reasoning, and in order to survive he spends more time acting on instinct than on any kind of conscious thinking.

This leads some to decide that the horse is stupid, when in fact he simply has totally different priorities to us. Try turning the tables for a moment: what if the horse took you into his world and asked you to function on his terms – just how 'intelligent' would *you* look to *him*?

A horse is extremely clever *at being a horse*, and we need to look at his responses from this perspective if they are to make any sense. For example, a horse may spook and run a short distance from a scary object that suddenly appears in his rear vision, then turn to look and check what it is. This is an entirely appropriate response for a horse:

1) This Arabian gelding has never encountered a beach ball before! The various facets of his body language – muscle tension, head and tail carriage, position and focus of his ears and eyes, direction of movement and so on – give us information about his emotional state. Here he is wary, but not completely terrified, and also just a tiny bit curious. He keeps his options open, eyeing up both the ball and his potential escape route…

2) …which he then uses as the wind lifts the ball into the air and towards him. His muscles are tense, ready for full flight at a moment's notice if necessary.

• The moving object could be a predator, so he'd better get out of there quick.

• However, he must limit the distance covered to conserve his energy, in case it is needed again soon afterwards when another danger threatens.

• Limiting the distance for which he runs also reduces the time taken away from eating.

• Turning to check means he can return to eating immediately if there is no danger.

To a person riding the horse, however, it may appear that the horse ran 'for no reason at all' (they could not see the danger behind – see page 9) and is therefore 'stupid'. Letting go of such ideas and trying instead to see matters from the horse's point of view is crucial in horsekeeping, training and riding. Instead of berating the horse for his 'dangerous and irrational' behaviour, it allows us to see that the solution to such situations lies rather in educating the horse to feel that when he is with his rider, whatever happens, no harm will come to him (see Chapters 3 and 4).

Can a horse think? Learn? Feel?

The horse *can* think, and perhaps reason to some degree: his cortex (the 'thinking' part of the brain) is quite well developed, and he can certainly learn to override his instincts if motivated to do so. If horses were unable to do this, we would have no hope of training them.

Even in feral horses, not all behaviours are instinctual or pre-programmed (see page 33). The horse has an excellent memory and often learns in one trial. This is a survival strategy for a prey animal – the horse that does not quickly learn that the bushes near the watering hole may be hiding a predator is a dead horse.

Horses use trial-and-error learning for real; we mostly do it in our heads. The horse cannot 'see' the solution to a problem facing him by employing complex thought. Instead:

• The horse tries out various options until he finds one that 'works' – it makes him comfortable and keeps him safe (see page 30).

• The action may be repeated a number of times, perhaps over an extended period, with the same result.

3) When he has put a little more distance between himself and the ball, the horse feels safer and relaxes slightly. He keeps moving, though, circling the ball at a lively trot.

4) The ball has blown into the corner of the arena and the horse appears to be ignoring it as he trots away, but his right ear still keeps it under surveillance. (continued overleaf)

• Once the horse has found an 'answer' that works, he will tend to stick with it unless there is a very good reason to change.

Establishing such habitual behaviour patterns is another important survival strategy in horses. Understanding how they learn, and how difficult it can be for them to unlearn, is one of the keys to successful training (see pages 95–99).

Like us, horses have emotional responses to events, but what these are can only be interpreted from their behaviour. This is necessarily subjective, although most people who spend time with horses should be able to recognize a horse that is fearful or one that is angry. Some other states may be more difficult to discern; for example, horses are often described as 'excited' when 'extremely anxious' might be nearer the mark.

Crossing the divide

Despite all the differences, horses can learn to relate to, communicate with and learn from humans, because they live and acquire social skills within the structure of a herd. Co-operation, personal space, control of movement, trust and respect – in short, the social 'rules' – are all concepts with which a horse living with others is extremely familiar. Luckily, they are also what we need him to know about when we start working with him.

5) When the horse starts to realize that the ball is not going to attack him, curiosity begins to overcome fear and he approaches the ball for a closer look.

6) He stretches out his neck to enable him to investigate it by smell, while keeping his feet at a distance that will allow him to escape at a moment's notice.

7

7) Although tension still shows in his muscles, the horse is now able to stand closer to the ball. His expression is full of interest in the alien object.

HERD LIFE

Horses are social animals that live in family groups. Understanding the structure of these groups, how the members communicate with each other and what is important to them is crucial if we wish to train horses in a way that makes sense to them and achieves co-operation and harmony between horse and rider.

How do we know?

There are no truly wild horses left in the world today. However, in many locations there are still herds of feral horses living in ways close to those of their wild ancestors, and detailed studies of these animals have provided invaluable information on how horse society works. In addition, domestic groups kept in as near natural herd conditions as possible provide a bridge in knowledge between the life of a wild horse and what might be applicable to the horse in our paddock.

The behaviour of groups of horses living in different locations is very similar, but there are – sometimes significant – differences according to the size of the group and its accumulated knowledge of the area, the type of terrain and climate, food availability, human interventions and so on. Despite this, we can draw some conclusions about what kind of animals horses are and how they lead their lives.

What kind of animal is a horse?

A prey animal

The horse is a prey species whose overriding motivation is survival, closely followed by reproduction. To survive, the horse needs first to stay safe from predators, and second to find enough food to eat and water to drink.

In order to reproduce, mechanisms must be in place that allow for successful mating and the raising of young.

A flight animal

As we have seen, the horse is a flight animal that uses speed and stamina as his first line of defence against predators. Only if he cannot escape will he stand and fight. The implications of these simple facts are crucial in training:

• Given the choice, when he feels pressure or discomfort of any kind, whether physical, mental or emotional, the horse will choose to move in some way until he feels at ease once again. This is his hardwired survival strategy.

• If that choice is denied, the horse may eventually defend himself – and then his speed of reaction and movement, large size and sheer power can make him dangerous to be around.

Working with the first option makes horses extremely easy to train. Pushing them into the second – and with some horses it doesn't take very much – can be disastrous (see pages 178–179).

▷ 10%

▷ 10%

A social animal

Unlike some zebras (*Equus grevyi* and *E. asinus*), which are territorial and largely solitary, horses and ponies (*E. caballus*) are social animals that form family groups or harems (see page 32). Each group will have a range over which they roam that overlaps with those of other groups. Such a range may cover up to 50sqkm (20sq miles), so *any* field we can offer must appear small to them.

A moving animal

Horses live in the open spaces of grass-covered plains and move almost constantly while grazing. This slow but sustained movement may be punctuated by occasional fast bursts, such as when youngsters are playing or the group perceives that danger threatens.

As well as spending the bulk of their time eating, horses that are free to choose tend to divide up their day in a fairly consistent pattern:
- Eating – 60 per cent (16 hours).
- Standing (avoiding flies and midges in summer, sheltering in winter) – 20 per cent (4½ hours).
- Lying down – 10 per cent (2½ hours).
- Other (drinking, socializing, breeding, avoiding danger) – 10 per cent (1 hour).

If food is scarce, horses do not increase the time they spend eating. If they are unable to move to better grazing, they simply become thin.

Understanding how horses would choose to spend their time will help us to devise appropriate environments and regimes in which to keep them in domestication (see Chapter 2).

Day and night

In hot weather, horses rest during the middle of the day. The group will close up more at dusk and during the night, as predators hunt at cooler times and when the light is fading. With more movement around them, the herd will be on higher alert for danger.

▷ **20%**

▷ **60%**

Social structure

Most of us are aware that horses live in herds, but over the years there have been many misconceptions as to why this is so, how big a natural group might be and the way in which it is organized.

Why do horses live in groups?

As prey animals, horses gain a number of advantages from living in groups:

• There is safety in numbers – it is much more difficult for a predator to pick off an individual victim.

• At least one member of the group can be 'on guard' at all times, particularly when the others are lying down and/or sleeping, to give an early warning of any danger.

This domestic stallion (on the left) has lived with other horses all his life, and has run with mares and foals from the age of two years. Membership of the herd is relatively stable – the same two older mares have formed the core of the group for a number of years. Youngsters are weaned by their dams and removed from the herd during their second year (see pages 34 and 36).

• Youngsters gain essential knowledge from older group members about their range, such as the location of water, which plants to eat, where to shelter and where danger might be lurking. They watch and follow the other horses in the herd and then try out the behaviour themselves.

All these factors are important for survival, and as a result horses have also developed a powerful emotional need to be with others.

Who lives in the group?

Horses naturally live in family groups consisting of a stallion, several mares and their immature offspring. Stallions rarely seek to add mares to their harem, and total numbers generally remain at around 12 or fewer. In a some instances, it has been observed that when numbers increased further, a second, subordinate stallion joined to help keep the group together, although his mating opportunities were few and far between.

The ranges of individual family groups may overlap, but interaction between them is usually avoided. For example, groups may come together at watering places, but generally keep their distance. They do not naturally amalgamate to form larger herds.

Geldings

There is no equivalent of a gelding in a natural group of horses. In domestication, some geldings can be quite stallion-like in their behaviour and may herd or even attempt to 'cover' mares; others are less so but may still fulfil the rest of the stallion role with mares (see pages 37 and 55–58). Given the opportunity, some will even form a family group with a mare and foal.

Horses living in large all-gelding groups may show a high level of aggression towards each other. Groups of three or four are generally better, perhaps because they mimic the usual size of natural bachelor groups (see page 36).

If a gelding grows up in a single-sex group, this can lead to problems if he is later expected to live with mares. His stallion tendencies may come to the fore, and he will not have learned early in life how to conduct himself safely in female company.

Growing up in the herd

On average, feral mares produce foals in two out of every three years. A foal learns rapidly to follow his dam and suckle only from her. He also learns how to cope with his environment, and his habits form early. It is therefore crucial when handling a young foal that we get it right: we do not want him to learn something we do not want him to know, such as his own strength, or that he can walk through a person as though they weren't there, or intimidate them into handing out food treats.

A window of opportunity

It appears that certain equine behaviours (including some sexual, maternal and social aspects) may be time coded and the first year or so of life is critical, so if these behaviours are not triggered, the opportunity may be lost forever. This raises the question of nature versus nurture: how far is the temperament and behaviour of the adult horse standing before you determined by his genes, and how far by the social environment in which he was raised?

A mare and foal are never out of sight for his first six months, although older siblings and other mares with foals may 'baby sit' so that the dam can have more time to eat. Studies have shown that a six-month-old foal grazes almost exclusively when his dam does, while a yearling still spends 50 per cent of his time with his mother, even if he has been weaned and she has a new foal.

The relationship between mares and their offspring is the basic cohesive force in equine society. Bonds between the generations are more important than peer group relationships, although these also exist.

Learning the rules

In order to live in the group, youngsters have to learn and abide by certain rules of behaviour. This fosters cohesion, keeping the group together and functioning properly for the benefit of all.

As they grow, young horses test and discover the consequences of breaking the 'rules', learn how to communicate and co-operate, and find their place in the social structure. A horse that has had such experiences in a herd will be easier for us to train than one that has not (see 'The lone foal', page 36).

◁ **Young foals stay close to their dams and suckle frequently. Within a few weeks, they will begin to explore a little further afield and socialize with each other and any older youngsters in the group.**

1) In this small domestic herd, the mares allow their foals to interact with the stallion at around six weeks old. These ten-week-old foals are initiating the contact...

2) ...and the stallion is happy to accommodate them. The colt (in the foreground) is bolder than the filly and is keen for the stallion to acknowledge him with physical contact.

3) The filly (on the right) soon heads back to her dam, but the colt sticks around for mutual grooming. In fact, he regularly spends a proportion of his socializing time with his sire, sometimes imitating behaviours, although he most often plays, explores or hangs out with his siblings.

Playing

Foals acquire knowledge about social behaviour and their environment from the older horses in their group, but they play with their peers. This provides important physical and mental preparation for adult life. Colts play more than fillies, reflecting the differences in the roles they will adopt later in life: a stallion must keep his family together, herd them when danger threatens and repel intruders; a mare uses most of her energy for the business of finding food and water and raising her young.

With all this to do, older horses rarely expend energy in play. However, most stallions will spend time interacting with their foals and may even have an 'apprentice' – an older colt foal that follows the stallion around, sniffing dung piles and checking on the mares. Infanticide by stallions, which many people fear, is *not* a natural horse behaviour but a dysfunctional one. In domestication, this may be a danger with stallions that have been isolated from an early age.

Separations

If a mare is in foal again, she will gradually wean her current foal some time from about nine months of age onwards. (If she is not in foal again, she will allow her youngster to suckle indefinitely.) Even though he is no longer suckling, the weaned foal remains with his dam, so there is no emotional separation. Once the new foal is born, the mare will tell the yearling to keep his distance, but within a few weeks he will be allowed to interact with his new sibling. Contrast this process with the early, abrupt weaning imposed on the majority of domesticated foals and it is hardly surprising that stereotypical behaviours (crib biting, windsucking and so on) often appear in susceptible youngsters at this time.

Other natural separations also take place in equine society – youngsters leave the group (see page 37), a stallion is ousted, an older mare dies – but some relationships will be relatively long term, such as those between breeding mares. The separations that do take place usually involve only one or two 'personnel' changes at a time. These aspects have implications for how we might keep groups of domestic horses (see pages 56–58).

Raising domestic horses

Traditional ways of keeping mares and stallions and managing youngsters may have arisen for a number of reasons including commercial pressures, lack of knowledge, facilities or the inclination to keep a viable-sized harem group, convenience for the human handlers and so on. This has led to the perpetuation of a number of practices that are now regarded as the norm, including:

- keeping stallions isolated;
- mares living without a stallion;
- early and/or abrupt weaning of foals;
- youngsters living without older horses;
- single-sex groups.

While many horses may appear to adapt to these conditions, it is worth remembering that they run directly counter to the natural life of the horse. Anecdotal evidence also suggests that horses raised in more natural groups are calmer, easier to handle and more straightforward to train.

Pair bonds

'Pair bonds' – in the sense of close, exclusive relationships between two horses – do not generally occur in feral horses. Although breeding mares that spend many years in the same group may form friendships, these are offset to some degree by their powerful bonds with their offspring. In addition, in feral groups close relationships appear to change over time, and depend on circumstances. The 'pair bonds' between two horses that we observe in domestication – and which often cause huge problems when they are separated – are usually the result of the conditions in which they are kept: as a twosome on their own, or with an ever-changing group around them, or in a badly structured group (see pages 56–58).

△ **This horse and pony live together without others, and by default have developed a close 'pair bond'. Here they move in the same way at the same time, just as a larger herd would (see page 44).**

The lone horse

In a wild or feral situation, a horse will hardly ever be on his own. Herd life is the norm, for the reasons already described (see page 32). A feral horse that lives on his own for any length of time is, simply, under a sentence of death (assuming there are predators around), but there are moments in his life when he may go solo for a short period.

Time to leave

As we have seen, an equine harem consists of a stallion, several mares and their immature offspring. But what happens when those youngsters achieve maturity?

When a colt reaches around two years of age upwards, he will be on the brink of sexual maturity and capable of getting mares in foal. Eventually, this will not be tolerated by the resident stallion, who will drive the colt from the herd, sometimes with the help of the colt's own dam. The ejected colt may be forced to live on his own until he comes across another lone colt or a 'bachelor group' consisting of colts of various ages, into which he will be assimilated. A small group of male horses is therefore a natural, if fluid, solution to the problem of colts without a harem. In time, the most powerful colt in

The lone foal

In a natural situation, foals grow up surrounded by horses of various ages and sexes. They learn communication and social skills, their place in the group and the 'rules' of the herd; they watch and absorb maternal, paternal and sexual behaviours. It is therefore entirely unnatural for a foal to grow up with his dam alone, a circumstance not particularly unusual in domestication. In such isolation, the foal will not learn the essentials of herd behaviour, since his dam will usually tolerate antics – especially the invasion of body space – that would be quashed immediately by other horses. The result is a youngster that lacks the social understanding and co-operative attitude that will allow him to get along with other horses *and* make him easy for us to train later on. He has, quite simply, not learned how to be a horse.

Horses do not naturally live alone for any length of time; consequently the domestic equine has a herd instinct.

the group may claim himself a harem from an older stallion, who (if he survives the encounter, which most do) will then become a bachelor himself.

This mechanism may be due, at least in part, to the need to avoid inbreeding – and to this end mature fillies are also ejected from a stallion's harem (although a stallion may mate with his daughters if numbers in the herd have become dangerously low). The filly coming into oestrus may be the trigger for her banishment. A filly on her own will eventually be claimed by a bachelor colt or a stallion with an existing harem, so again she spends relatively little time living by herself. Fillies do not form 'spinster groups', so a group of female horses without a mature male is an unnatural situation.

Welcoming newcomers

Because of these social arrangements, a male horse will generally be welcomed into a group of other males relatively quickly and easily. Far more aggression and turmoil is displayed by a group of females if another female is introduced, and it will also take much longer for her to be assimilated. Conversely, bringing a stallion into such a group will, after the initial upheaval, usually *enhance* the level of social cohesion, suggesting that one of his roles may be 'peace keeper'. It is worth considering these differences in the natural behaviours of males and females when creating groups of domestic horses (see page 33).

1) Geldings meeting in a domestic setting investigate each other through touch…

2) …and smell. The chestnut is the newcomer and is somewhat distracted by his unfamiliar surroundings, but he is also confident…

3) …and soon settles to graze, while the spotted horse tries to figure out whether he will be allowed any closer to his new field mate.

4) United by a common threat: after a relatively short time, the horses find security with each other when disturbed by noise and movement at the edge of their field.

Is there a hierarchy in equine society?

Observations, ideas and theories on herd hierarchies, pecking orders, leadership, 'alpha' horses and so on have changed and developed over the years, and continue to do so as more information is gathered about the behaviour of feral horses.

Not so long ago, it was believed that the stallion organized and led the herd, stole mares from other groups and spent most of his time fighting with other males. More recently, the 'lead mare' has been hailed as the central figure in equine society, with the other members organizing themselves in a hierarchy below her – those unfortunate enough to be at the bottom being most likely to be taken by predators.

The truth is not quite so simple, and some detailed studies appear to show that the social structure of equine society is in fact relatively complex and fluid. So what is it that holds a group of horses together and makes their society 'work'?

Competition and aggression

Ask most horse owners to identify the 'boss' horse in their domestic herd, and they will do so without hesitation: it's the aggressive bully who is first to the water trough, first to the hay and first to the gate, scattering the other horses out of his way with a furious look, pinned ears and the threat of worse to come if they don't move, *now.*

Such aggressive interactions between horses are immediately obvious, which is why we notice them – it is much more difficult for us to detect more subtle communications involving no more than the twitch of a muscle and a change of 'intent' (see page 42). Most importantly, these interactions are taking place in domestic conditions, where herds rarely resemble a natural family group and space and resources are almost inevitably restricted, so that horses are forced to compete for what is available.

In contrast, in a feral group there is little over which individual members need to compete: space is virtually unlimited, and the horses rarely display aggression over food even if little is available – they simply move away to try to find more. Living in natural conditions, competition and aggression are not major features of the daily life of horses.

'Alphas' and leadership

It was in domestic conditions, often in a laboratory setting, that the idea of a 'hierarchy of aggression' in social animals arose. The 'alpha' member of the group, and the hierarchy below, was originally defined by the number of threats offered by each animal. When this idea was later adopted by horsemen, however, the definition appeared to undergo a subtle change – the alpha horse was now also the 'leader'.

In reality, however, alpha horses are avoided bullies rather than trusted leaders. When a horse offers aggression, the other horse either aggresses back or moves away – no 'leadership' is involved here. Such interactions tend to weaken the bonds between horses, not strengthen them: alphas generally have few friends or followers.

Is there a 'leader'?

The answer to this question is a qualified 'yes', but it's not always the same horse. The role appears to be taken by different animals at different times and depending on circumstances. If danger threatens, the stallion will round up his family and direct them to move by herding them from behind. Other group movements may be initiated by an older mare, but not always the same one – and she need not necessarily be physically in the lead.

Some studies appear to identify a particular mare who has increased influence over group members, others do not. One factor that has *not* been identified in horses living in natural conditions is a straightforward hierarchy, headed by a single 'leader'. The dynamics of equine society are not as simple as they may at first appear.

Natural aggression

Aggression *is* displayed by feral horses in some circumstances, for example when:

- A mare has a new foal and keeps her yearling and other horses away.
- A youngster oversteps the mark (for example, by trying to suckle from a mare that is not his dam, or barging into an older horse's space).
- A new mare arrives.
- The group becomes too large.

The role of the stallion

Contrary to popular belief, a stallion spends the vast majority of his time engaged in non-aggressive activity. His job is to mate with the mares, maintain harmony (see page 37) and protect the group from any danger.

On the occasions when stallions do challenge each other, posturing takes place before a full-blown physical fight ensues. This allows one stallion the option of backing off before this point, helping to avoid injury to either. Once the fight is on, injuries can be severe, although deaths are rare.

◁ The older grey stallion on the right has successfully seen off his younger challenger, without serious injury to either party. Once he has chased him far enough that he no longer poses a threat, the resident stallion will return to his herd (see box on page 45).

▽ This group of feral horses make their way purposefully from a watering hole – but who is actually 'leading' their movement?

Affiliative behaviours

The roots of equine social behaviour lie not in competition between individuals (see page 38), which tends to split the group, but in the close mare–offspring relationship and affiliative (friendly) behaviours, which tend to produce cohesion. Affiliative behaviours are very important in reinforcing bonds between the various horses in the group and maintaining harmony. Such behaviours include:

• mares touching and licking their foals;
• mutual grooming;
• mutual fly-swishing;
• keeping watch while others rest or sleep.

One study of a domestic herd discerned a 'hierarchy of affiliative behaviours' – that is, some horses performed more of these behaviours than others. However, the assumption that horses that performed more affiliative behaviours would also perform fewer aggressive behaviours was not confirmed: while some horses appeared to fit this model, others actually performed more (or fewer) of *both*. Again, relationships and behaviours within equine society appear to be more complex and subtle than perhaps we might think.

A basis for training?

Some systems for training horses are based on, or at least explained by, theories about herd hierarchies, acting as the 'lead mare', mimicking the 'alpha' horse and so on. However, as we have seen (page 38), it now appears that many of these ideas may be too simplistic or in need of revision.

Either way, whether these theories are accurate or not, ultimately it is the interaction between individual horses – the ways in which they communicate their intentions to each other, define their own space, move each other around – that may be more relevant to training methods. Training is, after all, nothing more or less than the interaction between the trainer and the horse, in each moment.

▷ **One mare keeps watch while another mare and both their foals sleep. Such reciprocal behaviour allows mares to have some 'time off' from maternal duties and fulfil their own requirements for eating and resting, which helps them to raise strong, healthy foals. It is therefore of positive benefit to the herd as a whole and strengthens the bonds between them.**

Communication

For horses to live successfully in a social group, they need to be able to communicate with each other. In fact, horses lead relatively complex social lives that include subtle and almost constant communication. This doesn't always have to be deliberate: a horse can pass on information to others through behaviour that was not *intended* to communicate.

Vocalization

Vocalization may be the most obvious form of equine communication, but it is actually rare in natural groups as the sound would draw the attention of predators. This is a form of communication where there is definite intent, although the exact meaning of a whinny, nicker, squeal or snort is not fixed and depends on context – we cannot create a definitive dictionary of horse sounds, nor understand all the information they might possibly convey.

For example, a whinny is a contact call and an isolated horse will use it to try to find others. We could interpret this as: 'Where are you? I'm here.' When another horse comes into view, the first horse may (or may not) whinny again. As each horse has a distinctive 'voice', this may now be an identification call: 'This is me. Who are you?'

Body language and intent

Body language is the primary method of communication in horses. It can range from obvious and 'loud' – ears sharply pricked, head up, tail raised – to almost imperceptibly 'quiet' – a glance in one direction, the twitch of a muscle.

This type of communication is probably not always intentional. For example, a grazing horse may suddenly throw up his head and stare fixedly at the corner of the field. Most likely he has just reacted to a movement in the hedge and is seeking to identify its source, but his sudden action, coupled with his body posture and heightened muscle tone, communicate to other herd members that danger may be lurking and they should be ready for flight.

There are several 'layers' to a horse's communication:
• His general intent (flight, in the example above, but it might be affiliative behaviour, aggression and so on) is conveyed through body posture and muscle tone.
• The context (the horse stares at a particular spot in the hedge) gives these a more specific meaning.
• He won't necessarily get 'louder' in his body language (raise his head further, arch his neck and shift his weight back) or follow through with an action (swing around and run away) unless he has to – but if he feels the need to do so, he will not hesitate.

Horses not only read intent in each other, they can also interpret our own body postures and muscle tensions with uncanny accuracy. This can work both for and against us during training (see page 99).

(see page 99)

Interpretations

Foals and slightly older youngsters display 'mouthing' or 'snapping' to older horses. In one feral bachelor group, mouthing was still seen to occur in three-year-old colts faced with a dominant older stallion.

There are many different interpretations of this behaviour including submission, fear, need for acceptance and so on. In some cases, these may be more closely connected to the interpreter's preferred ideas about social structure and interaction in the herd – and related methods of training – than the intentions of the horses themselves.

The doors of perception

The well-known story of Clever Hans is a striking example of equine ability to interpret human body language. Hans' owner, Wilhelm von Osten, had apparently trained him to make mathematical calculations and tap out the answer with his hoof, but it eventually became clear that the horse was actually 'reading' the minutest changes in muscle tension in the people around him as he reached the correct answer. Von Osten believed himself totally discredited, but he and his critics had completely missed the more important point: if a horse can perceive the tiniest body signals so accurately, how subtle is it possible for the communication between human and horse to become?

▽ While this lioness obviously spells danger for the herd of zebra, their ability to detect even the subtlest signals of her *intent* mean that they are not in flight mode despite her nearness. They are certainly aware of her presence, but feel safe enough to continue to walk in the same direction as her. The lioness is a picture of nonchalance, but this scene will change in a second the moment she starts to hunt. We can learn a lot about how horses read us and our intent from an incident like this.

Taking action

If body language is not enough to get the message across, the horse will proceed to take action. For example, a youngster tries to drink at the water hole before a mature mare. The older horse might first throw a powerful glance in his direction, then pin her ears and wrinkle her nose, then snake her head towards the youngster, and finally bite him. At any point along the way, the younger horse could move out of the way, and then the mare would not follow through with 'louder' actions – but if she has to, she will do so instantly. Equally, once the youngster has moved far enough out of her way she will return immediately to a relaxed posture and start drinking: she does not continue chasing after him, biting him repeatedly as she goes. The next time, the youngster will move at the first glance.

This readily observable method of teaching and learning between horses forms the basis for many aspects – and even whole systems – of horse training (see page 95), but it is not the only way in which horses get their message across.

Synchronization

Let's go back to our example of the horse in the field (see page 42). He throws up his head and stares into the hedge. He's not sure all is as it should be, so his posture becomes more extreme and he rocks his weight back, ready to move. Finally, the bushes rustle again and he takes flight – and the herd instantly goes with him. As they gallop, twisting and turning around the field, the horses' movements are perfectly synchronized, and it becomes impossible to tell which horse is 'leading' and which 'following'. All members of the group appear to be doing this together.

A foal learns to synchronize his movements with those of his dam almost as soon as he is born; youngsters practise this daily with each other as they play. It is an essential survival strategy: when danger threatens, communication is instant and the herd moves as one. However crude our attempts may be in comparison, tapping into this type of communication in our own interaction with the horse can bring a whole new dimension and quality to training (see pages 113–114).

△ **The herd moves as one. In particular, the movement of the two yearlings at the back of the group, who were born within days of each other and are close friends, is perfectly synchronized.**

△ **This pair are trotting in unison and have spotted something scary up ahead. The older chestnut has reacted a split second earlier than his two-year-old companion, who instantly follows suit and matches his 'herd leader's' actions almost exactly.**

Personal space

Personal space is extremely important to a horse, and he will have no hesitation in defending it against those he decides have no business being there. Understanding the implications of this is essential to successful training (see pages 98–99).

A horse's personal space varies in size depending on a number of factors, including:

• **The horse with which he is interacting** Friends are allowed to be closer, and more often so; strangers will be kept well away; the dominant horse in an interaction can move the other horse out of his space; other horses may not even attempt to approach an aggressive type; and so on.

• **Mood** An older horse may tolerate youngsters approaching him to play one moment but drive them away the next.

• **Intent** A horse may welcome another entering his space with the intention of mutual grooming, but not if the same horse is trying to take a share of the only patch of shade in the field.

• **Circumstances** Maintaining personal space becomes secondary to the need to bunch up together during flight (so that a predator cannot pick off one horse so easily), or when an unknown horse approaches the group.

Horses usually like to spread out when grazing, but stay in visual contact in case danger threatens. Domestication often imposes conditions where there is not enough space, leading to increased levels of stress and aggression. Horses raised in restricted areas may have different ideas of personal space, and how close they need to be to others.

Stallion space

A stallion's personal space could be said to include the whole herd when a horse (particularly a stallion) or horses from another group approach. Once the intruder has left the stallion/herd personal space, the resident stallion does not continue to chase him down.

2 THE HORSE IN OUR WORLD

Horses naturally live and socialize in family groups, travel over large distances, prefer open areas and eat almost continuously. So how does a horse adapt to domestication, which often offers the exact opposite of these conditions? This chapter explains how to handle your horse's lifestyle in a way that is sympathetic to his inherent nature.

YOUR HORSE'S ENVIRONMENT

As soon as the horse is brought into domestication, practicality demands that the conditions in which he lives have to be modified – but the horse himself retains all the natural instincts of his feral counterparts. Setting up a living environment that will keep your horse happy and healthy *and* suit your own ambitions, time and resources is the challenge.

Some horses appear able to adapt to quite severe restrictions on their natural way of life. The majority, however, cannot and show varying degrees of unwanted behaviour as a result. In addition, some horses that appear to be doing fine may actually have shut down to some degree, as a way of coping with the stress they are experiencing.

Whatever the situation in which you keep your horse – in a livery yard, sharing a field with a friend, at home – it is worth making any adaptations you can that will help him to express as many of his natural behaviours as possible. Find the best compromise you can within your own situation between his need to 'be a horse' and the demands of domestication and the work you want to do with him. Both of you will benefit, since he will be happier, more settled, and easier to manage and enjoy.

The rest of this section discusses the pros and cons of various options, and the adaptations you can consider to your existing set-up to make your horse's life more pleasant. He will spend the vast majority of his time in this situation, so even small improvements – which is all that may be possible if, say, you are abiding by a livery yard regime – can make a big difference to his well-being and attitude to life. If you are in a position to make bigger changes – perhaps you are lucky enough to have your own yard and land – so much the better.

Two scenarios

Here are two hypothetical situations to demonstrate the possible extremes in which a domestic horse might be kept.

	WORST CASE	BEST CASE
Stabling	Small dark stable, no other horses in sight, confined 23 hours a day, long periods without food	Free access to a large barn, group of horses, ad lib forage
Turnout	Same small, featureless paddock all year round	Large fields with varied terrain and features (trees, rocks, stream)
Companions	Lone horse, cannot even touch others over a fence	'Family-sized' group of horses of mixed ages and sexes

Stabling

The first point to note is that a feral horse would not choose to spend time in a confined, enclosed space, for fear of becoming trapped. Even in adverse weather – hot or cold – he would never choose to shelter in a cave!

Nevertheless, most horses can adapt to spending some time in a stable, especially if they have learned to associate it with food. However, for the sake of your horse's health and well-being this time is best limited.

The balance between the time your horse spends in the stable and turned out in the field depends on a number of factors, which include:

- facilities available;
- weather and time of year;
- amount and type of work the horse is expected to do;
- your other commitments;
- rules and routine of your livery yard (if applicable).

Notice that, almost exclusively, these are for the benefit not of the horse but of the people looking after him, or are necessitated by the domestic circumstances; for example, the horse needs to come into a stable during the day in summer because his paddock offers no shade or shelter from flies.

There is therefore nothing that says a horse *must* spend some time in a stable for the sake of his health and well-being, but equally that doesn't mean it is wrong for him to spend relatively short periods there. Horse-friendly stable design, or alternatives such as yarding or communal barns, will help to ensure he remains as calm and content as possible while confined, so it is worth considering what changes you may need or be able to make to your current set-up to keep your horse happy and easy to manage.

Individual stabling (all types)
Pros
• Ease of management.
• Useful if a horse is unwell.

Cons
• Restriction of movement.
• No/limited social contact.
• Often restricted feeding (see page 61).

Possible improvements
• Make each box as large as possible (many off-the-peg are not big enough) to allow for plenty of movement, ease of lying down (even rolling), lying on unsoiled bedding, moving away from the horse next door if they are not friends and/or at feed time.
• Create extra windows (prevailing wind permitting) to make the box lighter and allow more views out.
• Use half-barred partitions between individual boxes to allow some social contact.
• Feed ad lib forage and a concentrates system that is closer to the horse's natural diet (see page 61).

Traditional stabling
Individual outdoor boxes in a line or around a yard, each with a half door to look over, possibly a window (on the same wall), and solid walls between the boxes.
Pros
• Can see other horses (especially if the boxes are around a yard).
• Can look directly outside.

Cons
• No social interaction.
• Very limited view out and/or of other horses.
• Relatively dark inside.
• Air circulation may be poor.

Possible improvements
• Make sure no box is positioned around a corner without a view of other horses.
• Add a mirror or (preferably) make half-barred partitions, or an opening (that can be closed off, or a mesh cover added, as necessary) between boxes.
• Add a window in the back wall (prevailing wind permitting).

△ **The windows in the front walls of these stables admit extra light but do not increase the horses' view outside. Solid walls between the boxes further restrict the opportunities for socializing.**

Barn stabling

Internal loose boxes along an aisle, often with half-barred front walls and anti-weaving bars on the doors fitted as standard.

Pros

• Ease of management (everything is contained under one roof).
• More horses in sight and in closer proximity, especially if there are two facing rows of boxes.
• May be lighter and airier if the roof is high, the end doors are kept wide open and the partitions are not solid.

Cons

• No view outside, unless the horse is in the end box (which provides a limited view).
• Possibly limited air circulation if the end doors are not kept wide open and the roof is not very high.
• A lot of noise and activity in the aisle at most times of day can be unsettling, as can people constantly petting horses on their way past.

Possible improvements

• If practical, remove the anti-weaving bars for a little more freedom of movement.
• Add a mirror or (preferably) make half-barred partitions, or an opening (that can be closed off, or a mesh cover added, as necessary) between individual boxes.
• Add a window in the back wall to provide a view outside (prevailing wind permitting).
• Make the aisle as wide as possible.

Converted farm buildings

Several types, including:

Old barn or shippon converted to stabling

Pros

• Easier to make the boxes the size you want, with partitions as you want, since they will be 'custom built'.

Cons

• Constraints of the shape of the building.
• Doorways often narrow.
• Windows limited.
• Roof often low.
• Often dark inside.

Possible improvements

• Widen the openings and/or make extra openings if feasible.
• Ensure that partitions are half-barred.

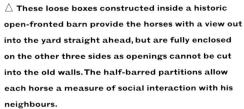

△ These loose boxes constructed inside a historic open-fronted barn provide the horses with a view out into the yard straight ahead, but are fully enclosed on the other three sides as openings cannot be cut into the old walls. The half-barred partitions allow each horse a measure of social interaction with his neighbours.

◁ Half-barred partitions and front walls are horse-friendly features of this barn stabling, but the view outside is very restricted – particularly as the horses cannot put their heads over the box doors.

Covered cattle yards divided by metal fencing/
gate systems, often into fairly large enclosures

Pros
• Light, open and airy.
• Lots of socialization possible.
• Movement not so restricted.
• May be easier to set up an ad lib feeding system.
• May be able to have more than one horse per enclosure.

Cons
• Danger of injury if a horse puts his leg through the fencing/gates.

Possible improvements
• House friends next to each other to reduce the likelihood of a horse kicking out through the fencing/gates.
• Fix boards to the fencing/gates to prevent leg injuries.

▽ **This yard of large loose boxes is constructed around a well-fenced central corral with sand surface. This provides useful 'turnout' for horses on restricted diets, recuperating from injury and so on, and can also act as a handy holding paddock when required.**

Full barn
Pros
• Horses can live in groups (don't overstock).
• Ad lib feeding is easier.
• Space for lots of movement.
• Modern barns are light and airy.
• Mucking out can be mechanized.

Cons
• More difficult to attend to one horse on its own.
• Danger of injury.
• Stocking level and make-up of the group are important, as is a wide entrance.
• A long, narrow shape (as in some converted milking parlours) is not as good as one that is broad and less deep (a horse is less likely to become trapped by others).

Possible improvements
• Provide access to fields so the horses have free choice.
• Adapt the entrance and exit so that horses can't get trapped.
• Open up appropriate parts of the walls to increase the level of air circulation.
• Add an individual enclosure or two for separating horses for special feeding, grooming, tacking up, illness and so on.

Field shelter

Pros

• Horses have free choice of when to use it.
• No restriction of movement.
• Light and airy.
• Horses can use it as a group.
• Provides a place for horses to lie down (if partially bedded) in bad weather if living out all the time.
• Ad lib forage may be easier to provide.

Cons

• May become a mud bath if left with just an earth floor.
• Needs careful positioning to avoid the prevailing wind.
• More difficult to attend to one horse on his own.
• A horse may become trapped by others if the entrance is too narrow.

Possible improvements

• Add an enclosure or two for separating off horses individually when necessary.
• Add proper flooring.
• Widen the entrance or open one side completely.

Yards

Connected to farm barns, or individual stables.

Pros

• Allows horses access to outdoors in bad weather without wrecking the fields or wading through mud.
• Access can be free choice, or controlled.
• More movement is possible.
• Hard, dry surface is good for horses' feet (see page 64).
• Outside individual stables, yards allow for more socialization (especially if the stables are very enclosed).

Cons

• Some surfaces can be slippery if horses are shod.
• Droppings will be distributed around the yard, so more work is involved in cleaning up.

Possible improvements

• Provide an appropriate surface according to how and when your horse(s) will use the yard.
• Add access from the yard to the field, which can be shut off when necessary.

◁ **This corral offers access to the fields behind, a well-drained surface for winter, a shelter, and large wooden bins for low-level provision of hay (see page 61).**

Think outside the box!

With an understanding of how a horse prefers to live, you can use your ingenuity to work out ways to improve your existing set-up. For example, if your horse has to live on his own you could:

• Run an 'alleyway' of fencing – perhaps electric – between his stable and field, where previously you had to lead him in and out, to give him freedom of choice of where to be (and reduce your own workload).

• Open his stable door on to the yard at suitable times so that he can wander around.

Employ some lateral thinking to come up with ideas that are suitable for your particular circumstances. Don't worry that what you do may appear unconventional or a little untidy if your horse will be happier for it. Always think through the safety issues, but also give your horse some credit for being able to cope with, say, how to find his way along an alleyway (as above) that may include several twists and turns.

Bedding

Bedding of some sort should be provided so that your horse is able to lie down comfortably to rest or sleep. You can leave some areas bedding-free, as it is good for his feet to stand on a hard, dry surface for part of the time (see page 64).

Unless your horse is on a very restricted diet for health reasons, don't worry about him eating straw bedding, as long as it isn't mouldy and dusty (when it is best not to use it anyway). He will naturally avoid the soiled patches, and it will provide him with low-quality forage to seek out and chew on (see page 61).

Noise nuisance

Feral horses live in a virtually silent world in which even neighing is kept to a minimum as it may attract predators. In contrast, stable yards can be very noisy places at certain times and this may stimulate horses to kick their stable doors, whinny, weave and even take a nip at people walking past. All this will be exacerbated at feed times, and/or if people respond to such behaviours (perhaps by shouting, or jumping out of the way of a nip) – a horse that spends a lot of time standing in his stable may be only too glad of this attention, even if it is negative.

A very noisy, hectic yard is unlikely to produce peaceful, easy-to-manage horses. Conversely, a horse that has led too sheltered a life in a very quiet yard may have difficulty coping with the inevitable hustle and bustle of the outside world. Try to strike a happy medium.

Stable routine

Contrary to popular belief, horses do not require a strict routine, although they will naturally set up patterns of behaviour according the weather (see page 55). However, once we impose a routine for feeding, turnout and exercise (generally for our own convenience), the horse will quickly come to rely on it and may become distressed if events don't happen when he expects.

A less rigid regime will generally produce a more adaptable horse – and can prove less restricting for you as well. For example:

• Muck out at any convenient time, rather than in the half-dark before you go to work.

• Feed forage ad lib, replenishing it whenever convenient, so that you do not have to be there at specific times to put up yet another haynet.

• In winter, keep your horse stabled overnight only in poor weather. At other times, give him plenty of forage in the field and treat yourself to a well-deserved lie in!

Such adaptations may not be an option if you keep your horse at livery, but it is still worth checking out what may be possible.

▷ **This old farm building has been adapted to provide versatile accommodation for two horses. The yard, which offers useful hardstanding and very limited grazing, can be accessed from either field, and one or both boxes if the doors are left open. This allows the owners to provide a regime suitable for both the small dun pony, who is on a restricted diet, and the young grey horse, who needs access to plentiful grazing.**

Turnout

Horses naturally 'live out' all the time and some owners aim for this with their domestic horses. Whether or not this is in the best interests of the horse depends on a number of factors, including:

• **Breed or type of horse versus the climate and conditions in which he lives** For example, a Thoroughbred may suffer if living outside in cold, wet conditions in winter, while a hill pony may go down with laminitis if put on to lush grazing.

• **Size and type of turnout fields available** Is yours a tiny paddock or a large field? Is the grazing rich or poor? Is the ground well-drained or waterlogged in winter? Is there natural or man-made shelter, or none? Is the field situated on an exposed hillside or in a deep valley? And so on.

• **Companions available while your horse is turned out** For example, if he has no companions when turned out and perhaps cannot touch or even see another horse, he may be better off spending more time stabled or yarded next to others, especially if they can socialize (see page 52).

If you can provide an outdoor set-up that suits your horse and takes these points into consideration, he will probably be healthier and happier living outside.

△ **The lack of stimulation and opportunities for movement provided by this tiny electric-fenced paddock may well cause this horse to invent his own 'entertainment' – such as chewing the wooden fence and/or leaping around when he is led back to his stable.**

▷ **The horses living in this gently sloping field have hedges and trees for shelter, and the remains of an old stone wall to negotiate through or over each time they make their way up the hill to the water trough. There are also far-reaching views across the valley, which provide the horses with a sense of security from predators that might otherwise sneak up on them!**

An interesting environment

While safety is obviously a high priority (see opposite), if taken to extremes it can mean your horse living in a very dull, impoverished environment where he never learns to look after himself, negotiate natural hazards, find routes from place to place that may not be obvious and so on.

Of course, you may have little choice when it comes to turnout for your horse, but if you have access to land that initially might look unappealing, it is worth bearing in mind that a more varied environment is closer to the natural life of horses – especially if they are able to move from one field or area to another at will (see below) – and will keep them happy and stimulated.

The skills your horse learns in this type of environment (see below) will be handy when you are riding. He will be more adaptable and used to a changing scene, and will already have 'learned to learn' – all this will make him easier to train. The opposite is true of a horse that lives in flat, featureless paddocks where nothing ever happens.

Desirable features that offer very little risk to the horse could include:

• **Varied terrain** Might include some flat, some undulating; some grassy, some gravelly and so on. This helps greatly with physical fitness, muscle development and balance.

• **Trees** Hedging, trees and shrubs are good for shelter, and perhaps a small wooded area through which the horses must find their own routes.

△ **Keeping horses with another species can be a good option. This stallion and two quiet rams are used to living together and co-exist peacefully, although the horse can move the sheep whenever he pleases.**

• **Rocks** While rocky areas that provide traps for unwary horses' feet should be avoided, you may be surprised at how quickly your horse becomes adept at negotiating less-than-straightforward terrain.

• **Streams** Especially good if the horse actually has to cross it, and/or drink from it (make sure it is not polluted). Crossing water while out on a ride will never be a problem again.

• **More complex shapes/areas** If parts are masked by groups of trees and undergrowth, the horses will need to work out the 'map' in order to find their way around.

• **Series of fields/areas** If the horses are free to move around these as they choose, they will set up their own patterns depending on the weather – sheltering (from sun, rain, wind or cold), eating, sleeping and drinking at different times, all of which involve moving from place to place. This is exactly how feral horses behave.

• **Another species** The obvious choices are sheep or cows (without horns, just in case!). If your horse learns to co-exist with these, and finds he can move them away, he will be more confident when you meet them while out on a ride.

Keeping your horse safe

Apart from obvious safety hazards such as poor fencing, dangerous items left in the field, hidden rabbit holes and so on, features to avoid in a field for horses could include:

• **Exceptionally steep slopes** These are particularly dangerous if horses have to make their way to the bottom in order to come into stables and/or be fed, as the potential for accidents at speed is high.

• **Odd-shaped corners** This is where a horse may become trapped by another.

• **Deep, fast-moving water** Horses will generally keep well away unless they have to cross it in order to access grazing.

• **Dangerously boggy areas.**

Bear in mind that a horse that has lived most of his life in featureless paddocks may run himself into difficulties, at least to start with, in a more complex environment. In other words, the more we try to protect horses (from themselves), the more danger they may actually be in (from their own lack of experience). Having companions that are relatively clued-up will help such a horse learn how to deal with new 'hazards' more quickly.

It's your choice

As your horse's owner, it is up to you to weigh up the benefits to him of a more stimulating environment against the level of risk you are prepared to take.

Field size

Take special care to ensure that fields are big enough for the number of horses living there. Overcrowding, especially if it is combined with a shortage of food (most likely in winter), is a recipe for heightened aggression and possible injury. Plenty of space also allows horses to:

• roll and lie down free from harassment;

• run around, buck and kick when they feel like playing;

• choose who they want to be near and who to avoid.

If you cannot provide interesting fields, at least provide the largest fields you can. This may be the most appropriate solution for larger, more highly bred and perhaps very valuable horses. These animals often grow up in over-protected regimes, may have difficulty dealing with complex terrain because of their size, and perhaps have less in-bred ability to work out problems than, say, native pony types.

Social life

Once horses are brought into domestication, there is no one perfect group size or composition that will work for every horse – and every owner – in every environment. There are advantages and disadvantages to every combination. Once you understand these you will be able to make informed choices about the best way to give your horse the social life he needs within the constraints of your situation.

Lone horse

Pros
• May be easier for you to manage.
• You may only be able to afford one horse.
• Avoids the downside of the horse forming a strong attachment to another.
• It is livery policy (to avoid injury, difficulty of individual feeding and so on), often using small electric-fenced paddocks.

Cons
• Totally unnatural (although a small minority of horses *appear* to adapt to this life quite well).
• There is no other herd member to keep guard, so the horse may not rest.
• No opportunity for social/physical contact.
• Horse may be dangerous if later put in with other horses, as he does not know how cope and fear can lead to aggression.
• Horse may latch on to others when out riding.

Possible improvements
• Make sure other horses are always in sight.
• Allow safe interaction over a fence (so it cannot be electric).
• Provide another companion species.
• Provide a larger and/or more interesting field.
• Ride with other horses.
• Spend more time with him yourself.

Pair of horses

Pros
• Some social/physical interaction.
• Easier to manage than a larger group for feeding and so on.

Cons
• Horses bond very closely, so may become distressed when separated (for example, when one is to be ridden).
• Unnaturally small group, so the range of social interactions is very restricted.
• Generally one horse will push the other around (especially over food), so neither gets the chance to experience a different social status.
• If space is limited, injuries may be inflicted.

Possible improvements
• Make sure the field is big enough to allow each horse plenty of personal space.
• Plenty of grazing and ad lib forage (if appropriate on health grounds) will help to reduce bullying.
• Teach the horses to be separated for gradually increasing periods, starting with just a few minutes (it may take some time for the horses to accept this calmly).

Membership matters

Groups of feral horses are relatively stable (see page 34) and this is undoubtedly the most peaceful way to keep a domestic group. Inevitably, however, some domestic horses may see the members of their group change relatively frequently and this can be quite disruptive. On the plus side, horses that experience this many times generally learn over time to react to such changes in a more measured way.

△ **The horses in this group range from one to 14 years old, and include fillies, mares and geldings. An older gelding (left) keeps watch while most of the horses graze quietly, and a couple of youngsters (right) practise moving each other around. The three yearlings (centre) lived together as foals and are often found closely grouped, usually near the older gelding, who appears to fulfil the role of stallion.**

Larger groups

Pros

• More like a natural group (especially if it includes a range of ages and sexes), with a wider range of social/physical interactions possible – large groups tend to split into smaller 'family-sized' groups, so enough space is essential.

• Easier to take one or more horses out of the field without causing distress to others, even if two close friends are separated.

• Horses will experience both moving others around and being moved themselves (which can make training easier).

Cons

• More difficult to get horses in and out safely.

• Injuries may be more likely, especially if food and/or space are limited, or there is not enough room for a very large group to split.

• More difficult to feed in the field.

• Introducing new horses can cause disruption for a few days, with the potential for injuries (see box).

Possible improvements

• Make sure the field really is big enough to allow horses their personal space.

• Plenty of grazing and ad lib forage (if appropriate on health grounds) will help reduce aggression between horses and danger to people feeding them.

• Train all horses in the group not to crowd people or other horses that are being led, or around the gate as you go in and out (see panel, right).

Single-sex groups

Pros

• Geldings together tend to be quite peaceful (bachelor groups are a natural phenomenon – see page 36), and certainly more peaceful than mares, unless the group is too big.

• Eliminates the possibility of some geldings behaving like stallions, rounding up mares and keeping other horses and/or people away from them.

• Eliminates possible disruption when mares come in season (at which time some geldings may be reluctant to be separated from flirtatious mares, behave more like stallions and consequently lose condition).

• Allows a young colt to be kept in a group without the danger of him getting mares in foal.

Setting boundaries

If the horses in your field tend to crowd people at the gate, coming to catch members of the herd, delivering hay and so on, for safety's sake you need to show them that they should to keep their distance.

First decide what space you would like, then define this boundary for the horses (see pages 100–102). You must be absolutely consistent in this, and make sure that every time a horse breaches the boundary you insist he steps back outside it. Your job will be made easier and results come more quickly if each horse in the group already understands that humans as well as horses have personal space. If you are at all concerned about attempting this with a group of horses, get expert help.

1) As the handler brings the bay mare into the field she asks the two geldings that are stationed there to move back by walking towards them with intent.

2) They are slow to respond, so she swings the end of the lead rope. The roan is on his way, and the handler will allow the rope to fall still to reward him for moving.

3) The coloured horse now advances to greet his fieldmate, so the handler again swings the rope...

4) ...which causes him to rethink and move away, creating the space for the handler to bring her horse safely into the field.

As long as the handler gets her timing right, swinging the rope to apply pressure and allowing it to fall still to release that pressure (see page 95), with repetition the horses will learn to move back as soon as the handler walks her horse into the field.

Cons

• Groups of mares are not particularly peaceful – they usually need a stallion or at least a stallion-figure (a gelding) to settle the herd.
• Horses used to living only in single-sex groups may cause disruption if they then have to live with the opposite sex.
• Youngsters often grow up in single-sex, single-age groups in which they learn little about social behaviour, how to react to the environment and so on (see pages 35 and 36).

Possible improvements

• Ensure that mares in particular have enough space.
• Make sure the group includes mixed ages.
• Keep groups to around four or five horses (large groups tend to split into several smaller ones).

Single-age groups
Pros

• Easy management of weaned or older youngsters with the same requirements for feed, shelter and turnout.
• Plenty of opportunity for play with others of the same age.

Cons

• Totally unnatural grouping, with no older horses from which youngsters can learn social and other skills.
• All the horses lack life experience, so the group tends to over-react to what should be mildly stimulating situations.
• Colts/geldings and fillies are often separated (see above).

Safety considerations

• In a group of horses, injury is always a possibility, even if all reasonable steps are taken to minimize it. Weigh up the benefits to your horse of a more natural lifestyle against your willingness to accept the risk.
• Group living is safer for domestic horses if back shoes at least are not worn.
• Socialize horses into groups gradually if possible, especially if there is any doubt over a newcomer's previous experience with groups or he is known to be poorly socialized. For example, you could introduce him to one of the more dominant members of the group first, in a separate paddock, and when they are settled put them into the group together.
• Horses must be able to sniff and touch each other in order to sort out a new group dynamic: 'introducing' a new horse over a fence where they cannot do this will not work, and can be dangerous as a horse may catch his leg in the fence if he strikes out or kicks at the stranger.

Possible improvements

• Keep geldings and fillies together.
• Adding even one mature horse to the group will help create stability and structure.
• Mix one-, two- and three-year-olds rather than separating them into age-specific groups.

△ **Youngsters living together have plenty of opportunity to play, but may also find it difficult to cope with exciting or frightening situations if there is no older horse to show them the way.**

Individual preferences

Remember that your horse is an individual and the way in which he adapts to various social set-ups may be different from another horse. Observing his behaviour with other horses in various situations will help you to find the best solution for him. Knowledge of his background may also be useful: some horses that have been poorly socialized as youngsters may be disruptive and possibly cause injuries in a group; alternatively, their lack of social skills may lead to them being ostracized by the other horses.

FEEDING

Horses are adapted to eating tough, fibrous, low-energy (poor-quality) grasses and other herbs for around 16 hours per day. They will eat, rest for a bit, eat again, socialize, eat again, rest and so on, around the clock (see page 31).

Most of the plants the horse eats grow at ground level, though he may browse for short periods on the leaves, berries, flowers or bark of some shrubs and trees, particularly if grass is in short supply. He may also lick and chew at mud and soil at certain times of year, perhaps indicating a need for particular minerals.

The horse is therefore adapted to eat with his head at ground level – this lines up his teeth correctly, so that they are more likely to wear evenly. He is also adapted to moving around slowly and constantly while eating.

Feeding for work

'Feed according to the work done', 'Increase the work before the feed.' These old adages are spot-on. Depending on their grazing or forage situation (see pages 60–61), horses can do a surprising amount of (especially steady) work before extra feeding is required. Think for a moment about how far feral horses travel (see page 31) – admittedly without carrying a rider! You may think your fit, healthy horse has had a reasonable amount of exercise when you've been for an hour's hack, but in reality he has probably only just warmed up.

Today there is generally more of a problem with over-fat, over-energized horses than underfed, lethargic ones. It is not humane to overfeed your horse, as you may not only compromise his health but also induce behaviours that you then seek to correct.

Feeding cereals

Horses are adapted to eat forage, not cereals, so feeding high levels of these divided into separate feeds that the horse consumes quickly is unnatural for him and may cause a range of problems, including:

• Digestive upsets such as colic or ulcers.
• Stereotypies such as windsucking, which some horses perform directly following a cereal feed, thereby upsetting their digestion even more.
• Behavioural as well as digestive problems caused by a diet that restricts forage because the horse is getting extra nutrients from cereals – a stabled horse then spends many hours with nothing to do.

Feed your horse as an individual

More knowledge about feeding horses in a way that is appropriate both to their natural adaptations and to the work they do is becoming available all the time, and not necessarily from feed companies. You may find you do not need a vast array of different feeds and supplements in order to keep your horse fit and healthy.

Check your horse's condition

The best way to do this is to learn about condition scoring, which gives an objective standard for recognizing whether your horse is too fat, too thin or just right for the work you want to do. Your vet or an equine nutritionist should be able to give you details.

△ **He may be a 'heavy' horse – this gelding's breeding is Ardennes x Shire – but he is also overweight. Note the fatty crest of his neck, his large belly, and the deep indentation of his spine along the top of his hindquarters.**

△ **This horse is neither too fat nor too thin for moderate work.**

Most importantly, get the feedback from your horse: he is an individual with an individual metabolism. Monitor his condition (see box on page 59), energy levels and state of mind, and maintain, reduce, increase or change feed accordingly.

The horse at grass

Ideal horse grazing would consist of large fields (to allow plenty of movement) growing low-quality herbs and grasses. Small paddocks of rich grass, often artificially fertilized to make up for the loss of nutrients when manure is removed for worm control, are usually less successful. However, finer breeds that lose weight easily may benefit from richer grass, especially if they are working hard, although it may go to their heads in spring and often autumn as well.

Rich versus poor

Horses on fields of plentiful but low-quality grazing will develop grass bellies in spring and summer (unless they are in sufficient work), but not deposits of fat along the crest, over the hindquarters and so on. They will lose the belly again in winter – this is the natural cycle for horses.

In contrast, horses on fields of high-quality grazing will develop bellies *and* excessive fat deposits in spring and summer, and their health may be compromised even if they do not develop laminitis.

Beware of pastures:
• that have been used for cattle, as these often consist of just a few species of high-quality grasses.
• on lowland and other soils that naturally grow plenty of nutritious grass.

• that are treated regularly with artificial fertilizer, as this tends to produce lush growth of higher-quality grasses at the expense of lower-quality species.

If you have access to several fields, a good solution may be to graze other species such as sheep and/or cows before and after the horses, which rotate around the fields. This will help with worm control, so you may be able to leave the horse droppings in situ and cut down on your workload. This system also spreads other types of manure over the field as a natural fertilizer, which encourages the growth of lower-quality plants better suited to horses.

△ **These hardy ponies thrive in their exposed moorland habitat, where the soil is thin and the grazing poor. Bring them onto richer fields and they will be prone to obesity and laminitis.**

Grazing for laminitics

Horses and ponies that are prone to laminitis may avoid it if kept on really poor-quality grazing (akin to that found on plains and high moorlands, to which their digestion is adapted), but can succumb on a small, apparently bare paddock or strip-grazed area that is actually growing richer grass. There is also some evidence that short, 'stressed' grass may be more harmful to laminitics than longer, older growth.

However, in most areas where horses are kept, the safest regime for a laminitic is a grass-free existence with low-quality hay as the only forage, except in the depths of winter. 'Dry lot' accommodation in a paddock of sand or dirt that does not grow grass – common in hot climates – is a good solution where practical. Movement is very important for these horses, so the area needs to be as large as possible, with the hay distributed around it. A wide, 'dry lot' fenced strip around the outside of a field (which can be cut for hay) is another option that will keep the horses moving.

The horse in the stable

The stable may be an unnatural environment for the horse, but you can still do a lot to ensure that his feeding is organized in ways that are as close to nature as possible. This way, you will be minimizing the chances of compromising his health and well-being.

Feeding forage

Forage should preferably be available at all times, otherwise your horse will spend long periods unable to fulfil his physiological and psychological needs to chew and eat.

Haynets, bags and racks put the horse's head and neck at an unnatural angle for eating. Providing hay or haylage on the floor is preferable (even if there is more wastage), as it lines up your horse's teeth correctly, opens his airway fully, stretches his neck and back muscles – and replicates how he naturally eats as closely as possible. This is not as crucial with concentrate feeds, as the horse spends less time eating them.

Feeding concentrates

We have already seen that horses are not particularly well-adapted to eating cereals. Molasses, which are often added to commercial cubes and mixes to make them more palatable, can also have an adverse effect – similar to a 'sugar rush' – on some horses. Various forage-based, unmolassed and cereal-free feeds are now available and may be suitable for many horses' needs, as well as replicating a natural diet more closely.

One system for feeding concentrates that may be more appropriate to the horse's natural way of eating is to mix small amounts with a good quantity of chopped forage in a large tub and allow the horse to 'graze' through it gradually over many hours. This may be a useful option if your horse is stabled overnight. Chopped forage with different nutrient levels is available commercially.

Snacking

A snack ball, which delivers small amounts of feed as the horse pushes it around the stable, can help to keep him occupied, feeding little and often, and 'searching' for food at ground level – but is not a substitute for forage.

Water

Feral horses drink daily if possible and are adapted to travelling quite long distances to water, especially at times of year when grazing is sparse and they have to move further from water in order to get sufficient to eat. One study observed a herd moving up to 60km (37 miles) between their grazing and water source.

Horses can go longer than a day without water if the weather is not too hot and they are not working hard. However, the most humane (and efficient) approach to providing water for domestic horses is to have it available at all times – then the horse can make his choice of when to drink. Conversely, you need not worry unduly if your horse has to be without water for periods of up to several hours, weather and work permitting.

◁ **There is no shortage of water for horses in the French Camargue, but feral equines in drier areas of the world often travel large distances to their water sources.**

SHOEING AND HOOF CARE

The horse's hoof is a complex structure designed to suit his natural lifestyle of travelling large distances generally at slow speeds, most often over relatively hard, rough, dry terrain. With this lifestyle, growth and wear naturally balance out.

The hooves of feral horses in wetter conditions, such as the Camargue ponies or native breeds in the UK, will adapt to cope. Instead of the short, compact feet of feral horses from dry climates, their hooves may be longer and will flare out and then break off as a way to regulate growth, since they do not receive enough wear in wetter, softer terrains.

Once the horse is domesticated, and we expect him to work in relatively demanding ways and with the added burden of a rider on his back, in most cases the balance between growth and wear will be upset. This is the primary reason for shoeing horses.

Effects of shoeing

Applying shoes to a horse's hooves is always a compromise. There are both advantages and disadvantages – some for the rider, some for the horse and some for both:

Advantages

• The horse can be put into work without any prior conditioning of the hooves for the new workload, without fear of soreness or excess wear.
• He can perform at optimum levels, over all kinds of terrain, even if his feet are sub-optimum.
• A horse with a genetic predisposition to poor feet can be kept comfortable and enjoy a useful working life.
• Shoes can stabilize feet that have become unhealthy because of disease or injury.
• The farrier takes most of the responsibility for care of the feet.
• The owner has only minimal hoof care to undertake.
• The horse is ready to ride however frequently or infrequently the rider wishes.

Disadvantages

• The rigid shoe prevents the horse's hoof from functioning as nature intended.
• It increases the shock transmitted to the tendons, ligaments and joints as the horse moves, and may predispose him to ringbone, spavin and other conditions and lamenesses.
• There is more danger of slipping on tarmac roads.
• Adding studs can help prevent slipping on some surfaces, but also increases the danger of injury to the tendons, ligaments and joints if the foot cannot slide a little when necessary.
• Various structures of the foot are no longer stimulated by correct function and/or contact with the ground, so may begin to atrophy, become distorted and cause problems over time. Common examples include contracted frog and contracted or underrun heels.

• Shoes can mask the effects of infections, deteriorating structure and early lamenesses, so that these may become greater problems over time.
• Nails weaken the structure of the hoof walls and allow easier access for the bacteria that cause infections.
• Loss of a shoe can mean the horse is *not* ready to ride just when you want to.

Shoeing options

Shoeing systems such as Natural Balance and Cytek represent an attempt to take the shod foot closer to the model of the natural foot and to help it function more naturally. A farrier who has trained in one of these systems will be able to advise you as to its suitability for your horse.

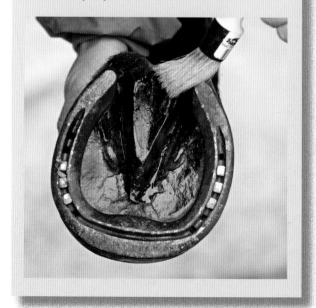

Keeping shod feet healthy

As your horse's owner, you should not expect to leave all the responsibility for caring for his feet to your farrier. Learn what makes a healthy foot and an unhealthy one, so that you are able to tell if your farrier is doing a good job, discuss your horse's feet with him and make informed choices. All farriers receive years of training but, as in any profession, some are better than others and you owe it to your horse to find the best one you can. With good shoeing, your horse's legs and feet should stay sound and healthy over his working life; with poor shoeing, you may run into problems sooner rather than later.

△▷ **This well shod foot belongs to a dressage mare who regularly competes at Prix St George level. Good farriery means that she is ready to be ridden whenever her training or competition schedule requires, without the need to condition her feet as is necessary with an unshod horse.**

Give his hooves a break

If your horse has problems with his feet but you would like or need to shoe him for work, a period without shoes to restore proper structure and function and give you the opportunity to treat any infections would be time well spent before replacing the shoes.

In this age of covered arenas and a wealth of different competitions and activities available all year round, many horses are kept permanently shod throughout their working lives. However, a period spent without shoes each year as a routine (as used to be common practice) will help to keep your horse's feet healthy, as long as they are still carefully trimmed and maintained. You can use hoof boots (see page 64) if you want to keep his work ticking over at this time.

Working 'barefoot'

Small children's ponies are often worked without shoes. The size of the rider, light workload and often naturally good feet make this successful without much special attention.

Many other horses can also be worked 'barefoot': there are horses competing successfully in dressage, eventing, hunter trials, endurance and even jump racing without shoes. In recent years, trims have been developed (mostly by farriers of many years' experience) specifically to help make this successful – a pasture trim is not suitable for horses expected to work hard. You must use a qualified trimmer, increasing numbers of whom are also farriers.

Your active role

Working your horse without shoes will avoid all the disadvantages associated with shoeing (see opposite) but brings its own set of considerations. Barefoot is not an easy (or necessarily cheaper) option. You must be prepared to:
• take an active role in all aspects of hoof care: your horse's nutrition, environment and exercise/hoof conditioning regime (see page 64).
• take the time necessary and put in the effort required to condition your horse's feet for the amount and type of work you want to do with him.
• be realistic – some horses may not be able to work without shoes. Sometimes this is inherent – hoof quality is not always breeders' first consideration; sometimes it is the result of poor foot care and/or farriery over a number of years.

Going barefoot

When you remove the shoes from your horse, he may or may not show signs of soreness to start with: the degree varies between horses, from no soreness at all on any surface through to some 'footiness' even in the field. For a comparison, imagine taking off your own shoes and walking over a variety of surfaces – then add a full rucksack to simulate a rider!

However, you should see improvement relatively quickly, unless your horse's feet were already in a poor state. Be guided by your trimmer as to what to expect, how much rehab is required for your horse's feet and the rough timescale to which you will be working in his particular case. Your horse will stay sore, or become more sore over time, only if he is asked to do too much too soon.

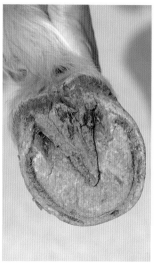

▷ **This horse's hooves regularly carry her through competitive endurance rides at distances of 60km (37 miles) without shoes.**

Using boots

Hoof boots in many designs are now available. They allow your horse to go barefoot, with all the advantages conferred by the foot functioning naturally but without risking excess wear or soreness.

Boots can be used during rehab and then for riding until your horse's feet are up to the work required. They are also useful for longer rides, if you know you will be crossing stony ground, or just on your horse's front feet if these are taking longer to condition than the backs (which is often the case).

△ **Hoof boot design is advancing rapidly, providing a versatile option for horses that are working regularly.**

Caring for your barefoot horse

Once a working horse is barefoot, you will need to keep his feet in good condition at all times. The effects of minor infections, chips, cracks and flaring in the hoof wall, minimal bruising and so on can be masked by shoes, but in the barefoot horse will become obvious at an early stage and affect his comfort and performance.

• **Hoof care** Picking out feet, checking all structures, looking for early signs of infection and treating if necessary are all part of daily barefoot care.

• **Nutrition** The effects of incorrect diet, and especially too much grass or cereals, show up quickly in the condition of the feet of many horses once the shoes are removed.

• **Living environment** Ideally, barefoot horses need to spend the bulk of their time in dry conditions on relatively hard surfaces. This can be difficult (but not impossible) to arrange in some climates! Some lateral thinking, and unconventional stable/turnout set-ups, may be required (see page 53).

• **Exercise/hoof conditioning** Barefoot horses need to be on the move as much as possible to stimulate correct hoof function and growth, but too much work for the current state of your horse's feet will result in excess wear. Your aim is to improve hoof condition over time, so that a balance is achieved between the work you want to do and the ability of your horse's hooves to cope with and even thrive on it.

In all these areas, your trimmer should be able to advise or guide you to specialist help.

Picking up feet

It is your job, not your farrier's or trimmer's, to train your horse to hold up his feet quietly for trimming and/or shoeing. You can use 'approach-and-retreat' (see page 67) to teach him to accept this happily.

1) The first stage in teaching your horse to be happy picking up his feet for you is to get him used to having his legs handled. If he moves or snatches up his leg when you touch it, keep your hand there until he settles and then take it away to reward him for the correct response.

2) Next, ask him to pick up his front foot for just a moment and not too high.

3) When he is relaxed about this, ask him to pick up his foot higher and hold it up for progressively longer periods, increasing the time by a just a second or two at each attempt. You are looking for a soft, relaxed feel in his leg before you reward him by putting it down.

4) If you are at all concerned that your horse may kick when you handle his hindlegs, use a 'hand on a stick' (or similar) as an extension to your arm, so that you can stay out of harm's way and not be forced to retreat at the wrong moment. Start high up on the leg, where the horse is likely to be more comfortable with the touch of the 'hand'...

5) ...and use approach and retreat to work your way gradually down the leg. If the horse snatches up his leg, keep the 'hand' there until he relaxes.

6) Move on down the leg, and do not think about picking up the foot until the horse can stand relaxed, without lifting his leg, as you move the 'hand' all over it.

7) Pick up the foot as for the foreleg, initially for just a moment and not too high.

8) Eventually you will be able to lift the leg higher and for longer periods, and take it out behind the horse for picking out. Once your horse is completely happy with the whole process, which may take a number of sessions, you can practise actions that simulate those the farrier will perform – such as tapping the hoof with a hoofpick and then perhaps a small, lightweight hammer, to mimic banging nails into a shoe – to prepare your horse for his visit.

GROOMING, CLIPPING AND RUGS

A neatly clipped and beautifully groomed horse is pleasing to most people's eye – but is it what the horse would choose for himself? Making informed decisions about what is best for your horse means taking a look at these aspects of care from *his* point of view.

The horse's coat and grooming

Horses in temperate climates naturally grow a thick coat for winter and shed it for summer. In warm weather, the short coat keeps the horse cooler. If he becomes too hot, he will sweat: this would be a difficult and uncomfortable experience if the coat were thick. In winter, in cold, dry weather the thick coat stands on end to trap warm air; in wet weather, the horse protects himself with a good layer of mud!

Why the horse grooms himself

Mutual grooming between horses is important socially (see page 40), but also provides relief from itching and skin irritations in limited areas of each horse's body. The horse can also 'self-groom' by bending around to attack itchy spots with his teeth or back hooves. In addition, he may use trees, fence posts, stable doorframes and so on as convenient scratching posts. He will be particularly itchy when changing his coat.

△ **This hardy unrugged horse can regulate his temperature through a variety of winter weather. His rugged companion may become uncomfortably warm on a sunny day.**

At just a few days old, this foal is able to relieve her own itchy spots by bending right around and using her teeth.

Rolling

This is a favourite equine activity, and not only for social reasons (see page 19).

- Rolling gives the horse's body a good physical workout.
- It provides instant relief from itches and skin irritations.
- When the horse is sweaty, rolling traps dust in the grease of the coat, helping to dry off the sweat.
- A layer of mud provides extra protection against the weather in winter.

△ **Horses enjoy rolling in both winter and summer. This small pony relishes relieving his itches.**

Why we groom the horse

We generally think of grooming as the thorough cleaning of the horse's coat, mane, tail and hooves using a set of brushes and other tools. In this sense, the only grooming that is essential from the point of view of the horse's physical well-being is to clean any areas that will be underneath tack, to remove caked mud that may cause discomfort elsewhere and to make sure that his hooves are clear of any stones or other potentially harmful debris. Grooming to stimulate blood flow is unnecessary for horses that have adequate turnout, but may be helpful for those stabled for long periods.

All other grooming is primarily for the benefit of the person doing it: you want your horse to look good as you hack along the lanes, you have ambitions to win at the show, you are proud of your horse and would like him to look his best at all times. There is absolutely nothing wrong with this – the important point is to realize you are doing it for yourself, not your horse. If you do not recognize this, you may stray into areas where grooming actually becomes detrimental to the horse, for example:

- Thoroughly grooming and even bathing a horse that lives outside will remove protective grease and dirt from his coat, leaving him more vulnerable to cold, wet weather.
- Some horses (often of the finer breeds, such as Arabs and Thoroughbreds) are particularly skin-sensitive, especially in areas such as the belly or inside of the thigh, and simply do not enjoy being groomed vigorously. If you insist on putting your horse through a thorough grooming every day regardless of how he feels about it, it will not be surprising if he does not welcome your arrival. He may also begin to object to the process in increasingly defensive ways (see below).

Having said this, some horses absolutely love the attention and sensations of a good grooming, so if your horse is one of these, take the opportunity to spend time with him in this way.

Mutual grooming

'Grooming' your horse by scratching him in his itchy spots, as another horse would, is a good way to enhance your relationship – many horses will try to 'groom' you in return! This is time well spent: your horse will appreciate the sensation, and you have the opportunity to focus solely on his enjoyment rather than demanding some kind of 'performance' from him (even if is only standing quietly to be groomed) – this is an aspect often missing from human–horse relationships.

Difficult to groom

Very skin-sensitive horses do not generally enjoy being groomed vigorously with coarse brushes, as they find it extremely unpleasant. They also do not enjoy being brushed tentatively with soft brushes, as they find this irritating and tickly. There are various ways in which you can make grooming more pleasant for a sensitive horse:

- Allow plenty of time so that you can move smoothly and easily around him, rather than rushing through the job. Brisk movements may encourage him to move around himself and become increasingly upset about the whole procedure.
- Use long, firm strokes of a soft brush.
- Use approach and retreat to get him used to having very ticklish areas touched and brushed (see page 68).
- Put up with leaving some dirt on your horse in non-essential areas, at least while you are training him to accept being groomed, rather than pressing on regardless of his loss of calm.

Defensive behaviour

A horse that moves away, swishes his tail, or threatens to nip or cow kick when you are grooming him may:

• be especially skin-sensitive.

• have physical soreness in one or more areas.

• not have been shown that it is safe to allow human presence in his personal space and touch on all parts of his body.

If his defensive behaviour has inadvertently been rewarded, by the handler momentarily stopping grooming and even backing away or giving up completely, the horse will repeat or escalate his actions each time he is groomed, perhaps to the point where his biting or kicking becomes dangerous.

Using approach and retreat (page 67) can help to resolve such problems, but if you are uncomfortable with your horse's behaviour or it has reached the dangerous stage, you will need to call in expert help.

Approach and retreat

This is how horses teach themselves about scary objects: they approach to a distance from the object that they feel is safe, retreat a little if they feel unsure, approach a little closer, retreat again and so on until they are close enough to investigate the object through touch and smell and confirm it is not going to eat them.

This principle has many applications in training horses, both when asking the horse to approach an unusual object and when bringing such an object into contact with him (see pages 125–129). It is particularly useful in helping a horse to accept human touch and the feel of equipment such as rugs or a girth on sensitive parts of his body. If your horse does not like you grooming, say, his girth area, try the following:

• Brush your horse in areas with which he is comfortable, gradually working over the shoulder and towards the girth area.

• Brush as far as you can towards the sensitive area without your horse becoming uncomfortable (approach), then work back away from it so that you are again brushing the shoulder (retreat).

• Now work back towards the sensitive area, and this time take your brush a little further into the girth area (approach). If your horse accepts this, work back away from it again. If he objects, keep brushing quietly in this small area until he relaxes, then instantly take your brush back to a comfortable area on the shoulder (retreat) – this is his reward. If you back off when he objects, you will be rewarding behaviour you don't want, which may then escalate (see below).

• Keep working in this way until your horse accepts the brush reliably in this small area, then the next time you 'approach', move it just a little further into the sensitive area and repeat the process.

• Carry on in the same manner (not necessarily all in one session) until your horse happily accepts you grooming all of his girth area.

This way of working generally achieves rapid results, if the timing of your retreat is accurate and you do not try to push ahead too far or too fast.

1) This mare has been caught by the buckles on the front of her rugs in the past (see page 70) and now resents being groomed in this area. She makes her feelings known very clearly!

3) She then moves down to the shoulder, which is still acceptable, and then begins to work around towards the chest. The mare is now more alert, as the brush approaches the limits of her tolerance.

Trimming

A horse's forelock, mane and tail act as protection against weather and flies, so you should think carefully before removing bits of them. We generally hog manes or pull manes and tails because we think it looks neater, rather than for the horse's benefit, although:

• Hogging (the complete removal of the horse's mane hair using clippers) may help a horse that is suffering from sweet itch, by making it easier to apply treatments to the skin.

• Thinning and shortening a mane may help a horse that wears a sweet itch rug or one that is sweating beneath a very full mane in summer to be more comfortable and stay cooler.

• Clipping a 'bridle path' at the poll will help to prevent mane hairs being pulled tight underneath the headpiece of a bridle.

△ This photograph shows clearly the protective and water-dispersing functions of the horse's mane, forelock and 'beard'.

2) The handler begins to work towards the mare accepting grooming on her chest by brushing her on her neck, which she positively enjoys.

4) Using approach and retreat, within minutes the mare is accepting – and enjoying – being brushed in her chest area.

Pulling alternatives

Pulling can cause some horses distress while it is being carried out, and there are now alternatives available for thinning and shortening manes in the form of special combs. The result may not always look as acceptable to us, but the horse (and handler) will have been spared an unnecessary ordeal.

◁ This well-trimmed show horse looks very neat and tidy, but removing his whiskers and ear hair has implications for his well-being that should also be taken into considerations.

Ears, nose and legs

Ear hair protects the inside of the horse's ears against weather, debris and injury, so removing it completely because it looks 'smarter' is likely to be detrimental to the horse. However, trimming off any bits that actually stick out will not affect him in any significant way.

Because the horse cannot see what is at the end of his nose, his whiskers act as an important source of information for him (see pages 9 and 16). Removing them for looks alone is therefore a highly questionable practice.

Removing the leg hair (feather) from horses of heavier breeds may expose the lower leg to a greater risk of infections such as mud fever. Most of these breeds were developed in cooler, wetter climates where the leg hair provides some protection against this. However, if the horse is already suffering from such an infection, clipping off the hair can make it easier to treat.

Bathing

Bathing your horse (or even part of him) with the aim of getting him spotless is primarily for your benefit, not your horse's. This doesn't mean it's wrong, unless it causes problems for the horse – for example, in cold weather he may catch a chill if you have washed him and neglected to dry him effectively, or have turned him out unrugged when he no longer has the protection of the natural grease in his coat.

However, there may also be times when you need to wash off parts of your horse to allow for medical treatments or preventative measures, so it is a good idea to accustom him to the procedure. In addition, horses may enjoy being bathed or hosed when they are changing their coat in spring, are very sweaty or the weather is exceptionally hot. It is therefore a good plan to introduce your horse to the idea of being bathed or hosed in these conditions, as he is likely to accept the process more easily. As with grooming and clipping, try the following:
• Use the principles of approach and retreat to accustom your horse to being washed.
• Start with easy parts of his body and warm water – in other words, don't spray a freezing cold hose straight over his head!
• Make progress at the speed with which your horse can cope – do not leave teaching him to be bathed until you are under pressure to get the job done, perhaps when he has an injury that needs hosing.

Clipping and rugging

The thickness and quality of coat (and skin) varies between breeds and types of horse. Whether or not a particular breed of horse can live outside successfully all year round depends to a great extent on whether those who selected animals to create the breed over time – and continue to do so – regarded hardiness as an important characteristic.

Today, breeds are increasingly spread around the globe as enthusiasts import the horse of their choice, often from thousands of miles away. Even if a breed has been developed to cope well with the conditions of its land of origin, it may not be well adapted to the climate in other areas of the world.

Fine-coated horses

A fine breed, such as the Thoroughbred – which has been developed almost entirely for one characteristic, speed, and is not adapted to deal with the climate even in its land of origin – will require rugging and/or the provision of adequate shelter in the colder months even if unclipped and not in work. Of course, you still need to look at the individual horse: some Thoroughbreds are relatively tough, some cobs feel the cold!

Thick-coated horses

Breeds that grow better winter coats present the opposite problem. Even in light work only, they may need to be clipped to an appropriate degree to prevent excessive sweating, discomfort and loss of condition. Rugging may not be necessary if the clip is not extensive and shelter is provided.

Some breeds that are adapted to very harsh climates, such as the Icelandic horse, may need clipping in other climates, particularly in early autumn, to keep them cool on warm days even when they are not working.

Should I clip and rug my horse?

All breeds, including the finer types, will need clipping if the level of work is high enough to produce excessive sweating and loss of condition. The heavier the workload, the more extensive the clip will need to be – and more rugging will be required to prevent the horse getting cold.

Once your horse is clipped and rugged (or even just rugged, to keep him clean for riding), the coat can no longer act as a natural temperature regulator because it cannot stand on end, carry a layer of protective mud or allow sweat to escape (see page 66). It then becomes your responsibility to ensure your horse becomes neither too hot nor too cold.

Most importantly, when deciding whether or not to clip and/or rug your horse *check who will benefit:* you, him, both or neither.
• Large numbers of horses that fall into the middle ground – their coat is neither very thick nor very thin, their workload is middling, the climate is not extreme and so on – can enjoy the benefits of a healthier lifestyle by remaining unclipped and unrugged.
• Equally, it is unkind to put your horse's welfare at risk simply because the unclipped, unrugged, permanently outdoor 'natural' horse is your ideal, if your particular horse would benefit from a different regime.

Rugging problems

Some horses resent having their rugs put on and taken off. These are often the same skin-sensitive horses that dislike being groomed (see page 67), which tend to be the fine types that most need to be rugged.
• You can help your horse accept the rugging and unrugging processes using approach and retreat (see page 68).
• Be considerate in the way you put rugs on and take them off: flinging a rug over the horse, adjusting it against the lie of the hair and then yanking it off also against the lie of the hair is almost guaranteed to produce resentment in a sensitive horse.
• On the other hand, you should not need to tiptoe around, folding the rug to the size of a tea towel every time you want to put it on or take it off. Most horses can learn to accept a half-way house, where rugging and unrugging is carried out in a workmanlike but considerate fashion.
• Take special care *never* to catch your horse's skin in the front fastening of his rug. This is a totally avoidable mistake: try placing your hand between the rug and the horse's chest, and pull outwards slightly as you fasten or unfasten. This type of precaution can save your horse from developing the undesirable habit of threatening to nip your fingers as you work the buckles or clips.

Clipping problems

Many horses are afraid of clippers, whether it be the noise, the vibration or the feel of the cutting blades against their skin. As a result, such a horse can become very defensive about the clipping process, often leading to him being strongly restrained, perhaps twitched or even sedated. These tactics may or may not get the job done, but will do nothing to help the horse accept clipping happily. To help avoid such problems, try the following:

• Introduce clipping using approach and retreat, not physical restraint (see page 68).

• Build up to clipping for real in very small steps, starting with simply turning on the clippers at a distance from the horse.

• Check your own attitude – is it to ensure your horse is comfortable with every stage, or simply to 'get the job done'?

• Begin with easy areas, such as the shoulder, before moving on eventually to more difficult ones such as the head.

• Do not try to complete the whole job in one go the first time, unless your horse is totally calm and accepting – there is no shame in having a half-clipped horse!

• Keep the clipper blades sharp and well-oiled – your horse has a perfect right to object if the procedure is causing him discomfort.

Dealing with a horse that has already developed an aversion to clipping can be tackled in the same way, but if you feel uncomfortable with your horse's behaviour you may need to call in expert help.

1) The handler switches on the clippers at a short distance from this mare, and she responds with the flick of an ear.

2) The handler then switches off the clippers and places them against the horse's neck. The mare is a little more wary and leans away from the touch.

3) When the clippers are switched on the horse can no longer handle the situation and leaps back. The handler now knows the parameters of the horse's concern.

4) She begins again by switching off the clippers and laying them against the horse's shoulder. The mare remains relaxed, so the handler switches on the clippers, and the horse is able to tolerate the noise and feel in this position quite well.

5) Step by step, the handler moves the clippers up the horse's neck, closer to her head. If the mare moves at any point, or leans away (as here) – indicating some tension and concern – the handler keeps the clippers running and in position until the horse relaxes again.

6) This is the look you need in the horse – relaxation, understanding, acceptance – before you even think about starting to clip for real.

7) Once the horse is happy with the clippers moving over the less sensitive areas of her body, she is more likely to accept them in her ticklish places.

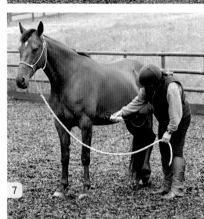

LOADING AND TRAVELLING

There are few things in the equestrian world as frustrating as a horse that won't load into a horsebox or trailer – and it's generally not much fun for the horse either. Far from being 'stubborn' or 'naughty', the reluctant loader is almost always confused and often frightened, even if it doesn't appear that way.

So, why might a horse refuse to load? The reasons vary, particularly between horses that are new to loading and those with more experience – although, of course, there is some overlap between the two categories.

First-time loaders

If you were an animal that lived in wide-open spaces with all-round views and avoided dangerous ground at all costs, would you walk happily into a dark, enclosed box accessed by a slope with suspect footing, at the first time of asking? Fear is the primary factor in an inexperienced horse being reluctant to load. The horse may:
• Be frightened of stepping on to a noisy, wobbly ramp.
• Be frightened of walking into the dark, enclosed space of the horsebox or trailer itself.
• Become afraid when the handlers rush to get him to load.
• Become confused about what he is expected to do, as the handlers give him conflicting instructions.
• Not understand how to lead properly, so is unlikely to lead easily into a scary space.

These fears can be overcome by:
• Teaching the horse to lead properly before even thinking about approaching a horsebox or trailer with him (see pages 103–106).
• The handlers being absolutely clear in what they ask of the horse and how they ask for it (see below and overleaf).
• Allowing the horse time to assess the situation, but keeping him focused and trying to solve the problem.
• Ultimately, offering the horse the opportunity to decide *for himself* to take the first and subsequent steps on to the ramp and into the horsebox or trailer. A horse will generally be committed to a decision that he has made for himself. If he has been forced, he will often refuse more vehemently next time.

Experienced horses

The reasons why an experienced horse refuses to load are many and varied, and include those listed for first-time loaders, plus:
• The horse's initial fears have been compounded by the (fearful, aggressive, uncertain, inconsistent) attitude of his handlers.
• He has had a bad experience on a previous journey that has left him afraid of entering the horsebox or trailer again.
• The horse has not been taught how to unload quietly and safely, so may have frightened himself on the way out and therefore be reluctant to load again.

• He has inadvertently been given a benefit (often many times) by his handlers when he did the wrong thing; for example, he steps to the side of the ramp and the handler responds by leading him away from the horsebox or trailer before re-presenting him at the ramp. The horse may then believe that this behaviour is correct and will therefore repeat it.
• The horse has been punished for offering a correct response. For example, he makes his first attempt to step up the ramp and the handlers immediately pressurize him (often with a stick or other heavy pressure from behind) to carry on into the horsebox or trailer, instead of rewarding him for his effort. The horse will then believe that stepping onto the ramp was the incorrect response and next time will try something else.
• The horse spends his time focusing behind him – waiting for the stick, lunge line, or whatever has been used to force him up the ramp in the past, as well as looking for an escape route – rather than into the horsebox or trailer. This makes it less rather than more likely that he will decide to move forward up the ramp and into the vehicle.

Human error

For both first-time loaders and more experienced horses, note that apart from any horse's natural anxiety over stepping on to the ramp and into the horsebox or trailer the first few times, *all* the causes listed for reluctance to load trace back to human errors in handling.

Tactics to try

There are many methods for teaching reluctant horses to load.
• Panels (such as the mesh panels of a portable round pen) can be used to cut off the sideways and backwards options without force, and will focus the horse solely on the horsebox or trailer until he decides to load. Moving the panels gradually closer to the ramp will encourage him to do so.
• If using a horsebox, take another horse in first and have a feed waiting in there for your horse as a reward once he has loaded (but do not bribe him up the ramp).
These two approaches can get the horse over his initial fear

A question of balance

Some horses have a major problem with finding their balance when travelling. This is often because they cannot work out how to move their feet while the vehicle is in motion; instead, they may fall sideways on to the partition and then scrabble frantically at the opposite partition or side panel with their feet in a desperate attempt to right themselves. This is very frightening for both horse and handlers, so it pays to teach your horse that he can adjust his feet safely by practising moving him around in the horsebox or trailer while it is stationary.

As long as your vehicle is set up to allow for this, travel your horse the first time or two in a larger space by removing the partition. If he cannot fall on to it, he will soon realize he needs to move his feet, and once he has discovered he can do this he should quickly find his balance.

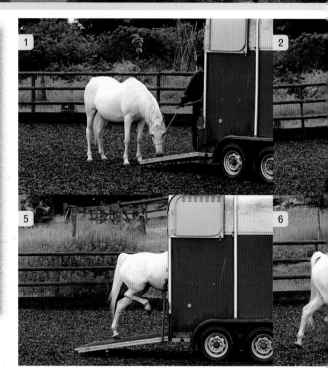

or reluctance to walk into the horsebox or trailer without pressurizing him, but will not actually teach him to load on cue, which is the ultimate aim.

To be successful, methods for teaching this to the horse require the handler(s) to have a good grasp of the principles of training horses, especially the use of pressure and release, and excellent timing (see pages 95–97). This is because you must reward every effort the horse makes in the right direction, and take care not to reward inadvertently moves in the wrong direction or lack of trying. Possible approaches include:

• Using pressure and release on the headcollar rope, working from in front of the horse.
• Using pressure and release (such as a swinging rope or tapping stick) to cut off the sideways and backwards options.
• Combining the above using two people – communication between them must be spot-on.
• Using a rope looped around the horse's hindquarters and back to your hand, to apply pressure and release from behind while you are in front.
• If the horse has been taught to move forward on a short lunge line on cue (see pages 116–117), using pressure and release from the side and slightly behind to train him to load himself while you remain on the ramp.

With a horse that has become a committed non-loader, you will need plenty of patience and a positive attitude! If you do not feel your skills are up to the job, or your horse is offering dangerous behaviours such as rearing on the ramp, you will need to call in expert help.

Travelling

It goes without saying that you should make travelling in a horsebox or trailer as easy and stress-free for your horse as possible. Make sure the vehicle is in good condition, of a suitable size for your horse and the suspension is strong enough to prevent excessive rocking. It is a good idea to travel your horse with an experienced companion for the first few times.

Some horses prefer travelling in a lorry to a trailer, or vice versa. An individual may also have a preference for facing forwards, backwards or diagonally, although many horses are very adaptable. If your horse is really struggling to settle while travelling, it may be worth trying several different vehicles in order to find one in which he will travel happily.

Relatively short journeys are best to start with, but if your horse is showing signs of concern such as heavy sweating, pawing at the floor or inability to find his balance, it is sometimes best to keep going until he settles and realizes he can cope. If you unload him before this, he will not have learned to relax in the horsebox or trailer and will have to go through the same process again next time, or may even refuse to load because he associates the vehicle with fear and confusion.

However, if your horse is behaving in a way that might cause injury to himself or you, or even a road traffic accident, such as attempting to get his front legs over the breast bar or kick his way out, for safety's sake you should stop and unload him immediately.

1) This older Arabian mare is a little fearful of the trailer. At the bottom of the ramp the handler allows her to put her head down and sniff it – this is how horses check out 'ground' of which they are uncertain, so initially it is a good idea to let them do this for a few moments.

2) The mare looks away, completely blanking the whole idea of the trailer. With her attention elsewhere, she is unlikely to respond positively to a request to move forward…

3) ….but, surprisingly, when the handler asks her to do so with a light touch on the lead rope she immediately steps onto the ramp. However, she stops before her hind feet have actually moved. Her attention is behind her (note the position of her ears), checking out her escape route. The handler's first job in this situation is to ask the mare to keep looking into the trailer and considering the problem she is facing.

4) The handler asks for another step and the mare responds by moving a foreleg, but her posture has become stretched and she has left her hindlegs behind, making it difficult for her to move them. This is a common situation with horses that are uncertain.

5) Nevertheless, the mare is willing to try and when the handler asks with the lead rope she unsticks one hindleg, and then the other. She is now able to get her feet moving and makes a big effort to step into the trailer for the first time. It is obvious that she is still concerned about the feel of the ramp and floor beneath her feet.

6) At the next attempt, the mare walks straight up and in, but she is stepping warily and has lowered her head to inspect the ramp once again, and the handler has mirrored the mare's actions by looking down. She would give the horse more confidence if she looked up and ahead into the trailer herself, when the mare would be more likely to mirror *her*.

7) The next attempt is much better. The mare is more confident and relaxed, although her ears tell us she is still checking that there is a way out behind her.

8) Don't forget to teach your horse to unload as well! The handler has her lead rope in a muddle and has lost the mare's attention, which switched to her surroundings as soon as her head cleared the back of the trailer. Consequently, she is backing out crookedly and at least one hind foot has to step off the side of the ramp. This may worry the horse, and make her more reluctant to load next time around.

TACK

Today, there is a vast range of tack, equipment and gadgetry available to every horse owner – but how much of it is actually necessary, rather than simply an attempt to paper over the gaps and misunderstandings in a horse's education?

Ultimately, the best item of equipment you have with which to train your horse is *you*. This is what Chapters 3 and 4 of this book are all about. In the meantime, it is worth assessing some of the tack you may choose or be advised to use with your horse, to see just what effect it may have on him.

Halters and headcollars

A horse that has been trained to lead properly – that is, that he should keep slack in the rope at all times – can be led and tied up in whatever style of halter or headcollar you like. You will not need to impose heavy physical control, because you have control of him mentally (see pages 103–106).

Halters for retraining

For a horse that has learned to pull on the lead rope, a standard webbing or leather headcollar may not be the best choice. The flatness and width of the material mean that the horse can lean on rope pressure all day, or even pull right away from the handler relatively easily.

△ **This horse is pulling back against the pressure of the lead rope, which he feels through the wide leather headpiece of the headcollar. He has no thought of moving his feet and is actually yawning!**

Rope halter

With a halter made from rope, any pressure you apply is concentrated on a smaller area, allowing you to use the rope more lightly and precisely, thereby communicating more clearly with your horse. This makes it a suitable choice for everyday work, and also useful for retraining:

• A horse that has learned to lean on rope pressure will find it's no longer so easy, and you can then start to retrain him to soften to pressure rather than brace against it (see page 104).

• With a horse that actually pulls away, you have a better chance of holding on to him, as the pressure he puts on himself while doing this will be more concentrated than if he were wearing a webbing or leather headcollar.

If your horse's behaviour has reached the stage of becoming dangerous, you may need to call in professional help.

◁ **This rope halter fits well, with the throatlatch passing behind the horse's jowls rather than over them where it might cause unwanted pressure should the horse pull on the lead rope. A thickish, slightly stiff rope is preferable as it provides an instant release (see page 95). A more pliable rope can hang more heavily on the horse's head even when there is no tension on the lead rope.**

Pressure halter/headcollar

There are several designs available, each of which tightens around the horse's head as you or he put pressure on the rope, and should release *instantly* as soon as the horse softens – it is essential to check that it actually does this. Such a halter can be useful in retraining a horse that, through poor training, has learned his own strength and is prepared to use it (see page 103).

However, it is a powerful tool that can exert a lot of pressure, so requires you to be really proficient in:
• The practice of pressure and release (see pages 95–97).
• Reading the horse (see page 99).

You may prefer to call in professional help, since some horses can start to panic and even be provoked into rearing over backwards if a pressure halter/headcollar is used badly.

△ **This design of halter tightens around the horse's nose as the handler puts pressure on the lead rope or the horse pulls back. This horse has learned to brace against the lead rope over a period of years – by using a pressure halter, the handler is able to show her that this is not her best option.**

△ **Any pressure halter should release instantly as soon as the horse responds correctly. The horse's expression has changed immediately and she is working her jaw. Interpretations of this action vary – from concern, to thinking, to acceptance – but either way, it is clear that the mare has released the tension in the muscles of her neck and face and feels far more relaxed than she did a moment or two earlier.**

Using powerful tack

When dealing with a horse that has been taught inappropriate and possibly dangerous responses, whether on the ground or under saddle, you may sometimes need to use powerful tack as a temporary measure during retraining. If you decide to do this:
• Make sure you are using the equipment for the right reasons – to help the horse learn, and *not* as a punishment or means by which to vent your anger or frustration.

• Check that you understand how to use it logically, consistently and clearly, so that the horse does not become confused and escalate his unwanted behaviour as a result.
• Be ready to move on to less powerful tack as the horse learns.
• Learn to recognize powerful tack that is designed *not* to teach the horse but rather to restrict his movements and/or disguise the effects of poor training. Lack of a built-in release is a sure sign of this.

Bridles and bits

There is a huge range of bits available and many designs of bitless bridle, plus combination bridles that act on both nose and mouth. The function of all is (or should be) to communicate with the horse: to signal to him what you want him to do, *not* to haul him around physically.

△ **This bewildering array of bits is just a tiny selection from those on the market today. As long as your horse is comfortable with the bit you choose, training him to respond correctly to it is more important than choosing the latest 'wonder' design.**

It is therefore your job as the rider to learn:
• To ride well enough not to pull on the horse's mouth or nose inadvertently in order to keep your balance (see page 132).
• How to signal to the horse through the bridle, to recognize a correct or incorrect response and to reward him when he gets it right (see pages 144–147).

Is bitless kinder?

Many people wish to ride bitless because they think this is inherently kinder to the horse. As the nose is less sensitive than the bars and corners of the mouth – although it is still a sensitive part of the head, and heavy-handedness can do damage – this will be true if you are using the reins to pull the horse around, or do not yet ride well enough to avoid jabbing your horse in the mouth by mistake. However, mechanical hackamores that operate with lots of leverage and/or tighten around the horse's face do not offer much, if any, advantage in this respect.

Learning to ride better, to communicate more clearly with your horse and to train him to respond correctly to a bit (and/or a bitless bridle) would be a better and kinder long-term solution. A horse that responds softly to a bit (see pages 144–147) will be more comfortable than one that is being pulled around in a bitless bridle

1) This horse has learned to soften to light pressure on the bit rather than brace against it. The rider picks up the reins...

2) ...and the horse relaxes her jaw and neck and drops her nose, giving herself an instant release by putting slack in the reins (see pages 144–147).

1) This design of bitless bridle tightens around the horse's head when pressure is applied to both reins. If you decide to use this or a similar design, always check that it releases instantly when the horse responds correctly. As the rider picks up the reins, the horse – who has never worn a bitless bridle before – braces her neck and tips her head to one side...

2) ...but she quickly generalizes what she already knows about softening to pressure and finds the release.

Keep him comfortable

Horse's mouths vary in size and shape, as do their tongues. To ensure your horse is happy in his bit:

• Find a bit that fits him correctly and allows enough room for his tongue (so that he can swallow easily).

• Choose one whose action is suitable for your horse's stage of training.

In both cases, you may need professional guidance.

• Make sure your horse's teeth are checked regularly and any problems resolved.

• Teach him to respond correctly to signals given through the bit (see pages 144–147).

Should I use a more powerful bit?

If you find your horse pulling, leaning on the bit, sticking his head in the air, tucking his nose into his chest or yanking his head downwards, and feel that a more powerful bit is required, consider first:

• Who is doing the pulling, you or your horse (see page 147)?

• Your horse may be losing his balance – he has been taught to carry a rider but not *how* to carry one, or he is at an early stage of training and is therefore leaning on your hands for support (see pages 162–167).

• Your horse is looking for relief from constant pressure on his mouth and has found it by shoving his head up or down, or tucking his nose into his chest (see pages 135 and 144).

• Your horse may have problems with his teeth and/or back, so that he is physically unable to relax his jaw, poll and neck in response to the bit.

It may be better to have your horse checked physically, then think about improving your riding and/or training your horse how to balance and respond correctly (long-term solutions), rather than looking for extra power from the bit (short-term fix).

Horses that have been poorly ridden over a long period may benefit from retraining in a different (though not necessarily more powerful) bit, combination bridle or bitless bridle that puts pressure on different areas than those they are used to. However, changing your horse's bridle and bit *without* also retraining correct responses may work better for a while but will soon have you back at square one! (For safety considerations, see box on page 81.)

1

2

1) This horse tries to relieve himself of bit pressure in two different ways: raising his head and pulling his neck up and back towards the rider, which immediately puts some slack in the rein...

2) ...and opening his mouth and leaning on the rein as he searches for a release.

Bridling difficulties

There are a number of reasons why your horse may object to having his bridle put on, including:

• Problems with his teeth. These should be resolved before any training solutions are sought.

• The mouthpiece of the bit does not suit the conformation of his mouth and thickness of his tongue, so is uncomfortable for him (see the box on page 79).

• He may dislike having his ears handled, or the bridle pulled up past his eyes, or your fingers moving around his mouth and so on. Isolate these operations to see which is causing the problem, then work on this using approach and retreat (see page 67).

• He has been inadvertently taught that sticking his head in the air effectively stops the bridling process, so this has become a habit that he repeats (see page 98). Teaching him to lower his head, soften his poll and move his head to each side on cue (see pages 110–112) will allow you to begin retraining him to accept bridling quietly.

Additional 'aids'

This category includes nosebands (apart from cavesson), martingales and training aids ('auxiliary reins' of various kinds).

A horse that has been trained and ridden well over a number of years, will have learned to:

• Pay attention to his rider.

• Stay calm.

• Respond softly to his rider's requests.

• Carry himself in good balance.

• Look to his rider for help in difficult situations rather than act on instinct.

△ **The picture presented here is completely different to the one below left. There is no need for physical control from the rider, since this beautifully trained horse controls himself.**

Such a horse will not require any 'aids' beyond a bit (or bitless bridle) suitable for his level of training. This is because *control* is not an issue – the horse has learned to *control himself* (see Chapters 3 and 4).

Trainers and riders generally use additional aids:

• For horses (and they are the majority) that have not had the benefit of this kind of education.

• When the trainer/rider does not have the knowledge or skill to train, retrain or ride the horse well.

• When the trainer/rider wants to progress the horse faster than may be appropriate to maintaining the qualities listed above.

◁ **Imagine what would happen here if the gag bit were replaced with something milder, and the flash noseband and running martingale were removed.**

Nosebands

Restrictive nosebands such as flash, crank or grakle are used to prevent the horse opening his mouth and/or crossing his jaw to escape the action of the bit. While they may succeed in this aim, these devices also have a number of disadvantages:

• A restrictive noseband may not allow the horse enough movement in his jaw for him ever to discover that he can relax and soften to the bit. Because the horse cannot find a meaningful release, no learning takes place and the noseband cannot then be removed.

• Combining a restrictive noseband with a bit that does not allow enough room for the horse's tongue and/or heavy pressure on the reins, can mean the horse becoming extremely uncomfortable and agitated because he is unable to swallow efficiently – excessive foam from the mouth or tongue lolling is an indication of this.

• By holding the horse's mouth closed, a restrictive noseband may disguise the fact that the rider is using their hands too strongly, as the horse's reaction of opening his mouth wide is effectively disguised.

Martingales

These pieces of equipment prevent the horse raising his head so high as to escape the action of the bit, and provide extra leverage and control.

A horse that cannot find a meaningful release – perhaps because he is wearing a restrictive noseband and/or the rider is using their hands strongly or incorrectly (see page 77) – may try the option of raising his head. This can be effective in providing some relief by putting slack in the reins, even if only momentarily, and therefore quickly becomes a habit (see page 98). A martingale may seem the most obvious solution.

Unfortunately, each time the horse raises his head up against the martingale, he is practising using his neck muscles 'upside down' (see box on page 165 for how the horse uses his muscles the 'right way up'). They therefore develop and strengthen incorrectly, so that if the martingale is removed the horse's tendency to raise his head is accentuated. In other words, the horse has learned the opposite of what we want, and the martingale remains in permanent use to provide physical control. Retraining the horse to respond correctly to the bit is the alternative, long-term solution.

Training aids

These auxiliary reins, which are available in a range of designs, are used primarily to get the horse working in an 'outline' or 'frame' and develop his musculature, either on the lunge or ridden – some are dual purpose. If you would like or have been advised to use one of these aids with your horse, consider that:

Side reins

Side reins do not have the same leverage effect as most training 'aids' and can be useful during lunging to help the horse discover how to soften and reach out to the bit. However, they are by no means essential and may also produce undesirable effects if used and/or adjusted incorrectly, so if necessary seek expert advice before using them with your horse.

Safety first

When training a horse to respond correctly to the bit and other cues, or particularly when retraining one that has learnt to respond in ways that may be dangerous (such as sticking his head in the air and running):

• Carry out all training in a safe place, such as an arena.

• Do not think about venturing out of the arena until you are confident your horse is willingly and consistently offering the responses you want.

• Expand the 'world' in which you are working as gradually as necessary to keep him calm and responding correctly.

• If you have considered or even tried retraining your horse, but really don't feel confident riding him without a strong bit and/or extra equipment, *don't*. Instead, seek professional help with retraining him.

• If incorrectly adjusted or used strongly, many of these aids can cause – sometimes severe – physical damage to the horse, as the leverage they exert can be huge.

• A training aid may produce 'outline' and development of the topline in the horse, but with stiffness and bracing rather than softness and release of muscles (see page 144).

• Trainers and riders that are skilled enough to use these devices without danger to the horse are probably skilled enough not to need them! The crucial factor then is *time*.

• Training aids can represent the ultimate shortcut or quick fix – the horse superficially 'looks right', but has not developed the qualities that over time would allow him to adopt this carriage *himself* (see pages 165–167).

Saddles

The primary functions of a saddle are to:
- Spread the rider's weight over the part of the horse's back that is most suited to weight-bearing – that is, on either side of the horse's spine, from just behind the shoulders to a point no further back than the last rib. The saddle should therefore be in contact with the horse's back all along this area and provide good clearance of the spine itself. Conversely, it should not fit tightly at the shoulders and withers or at the cantle.
- Provide extra comfort for the rider, particularly on a wide horse.
- Help the rider feel more secure – stirrups, especially, help with less-than-perfect balance.
- Help the rider with their position for particular disciplines, using specialist designs.

1) This saddle is too narrow for the horse and is 'bridging'. The pommel is sitting up high, and when the rider gets on there will be intense pressure from the tree at the front and back of the saddle. Beneath the seat, where the horse's back is best able to carry weight, there is very little contact between the panels of the saddle and the horse's back.

1) Depending on the conformation of the individual horse, the usual advice to position the saddle by placing it on the horse's lower neck and then sliding it back until it settles comfortably may not always be appropriate. This saddle has been positioned in this way and is too far forward – a sight that is not particularly uncommon. The seat is tilting up towards the pommel and the girth is very close behind the horse's elbows.

2) The same saddle is now positioned further back, which will allow the horse's shoulders to move freely (assuming the saddle fits correctly).

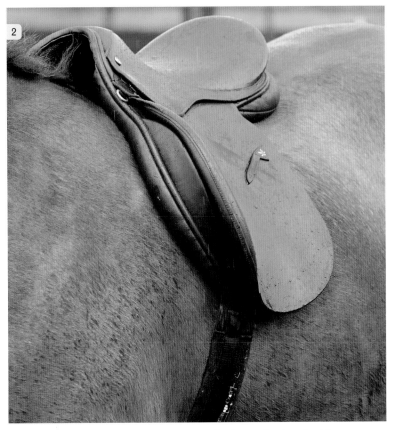

2) This view shows that the horse will have difficulty moving her shoulders freely, and will probably become sore where the points of the tree dig into her back behind the withers.

Saddle-fit problems

These can include the following:

For the rider

• The saddle puts the rider into an unbalanced or 'incorrect' position.

• Riders are all different shapes and sizes (and there are significant differences between men and women), so a mismatched saddle that makes an individual uncomfortable will have repercussions for their riding, and therefore for communication with the horse and even his physical well-being.

For the horse

• The saddle 'bridges' the part of the horse's back it should sit on and digs in at withers/ shoulders and cantle.

• The saddle is too narrow and has been fitted too far forward, so it restricts the movement of horse's shoulders and eventually causes muscle wastage on either side of the withers.

• The horse changes shape with the seasons, his age and his work, so a saddle fitted to areas that are affected by this (such as the withers and shoulders) may no longer fit. A saddle that is designed so that it is fitted to the shape of the ribs (as saddles should be – see above) will not be affected unless there are major gains or losses in weight and muscle.

• The front-to-back balance of the saddle does not match that of the horse, so the saddle rocks and causes pressure points.

• The gullet is too narrow, so the panels impinge on the horse's spine.

• The panels are mismatched and/or lumpy.

• The stirrup bars are set so far into the tree that they dig into the horse.

• The saddle is not symmetrical.

Surprisingly, none of these problems is particularly uncommon, so for your horse's sake you should work with the best saddle fitter you can to ensure that your horse is as comfortable as possible in his saddle.

Helping your horse

Some problems that appear to be caused by saddle fit – for example, asymmetrical rubbing or evidence of pressure beneath the cantle – may actually have more to do with the person sitting in it. Learning to ride as well as you can will help to keep your horse comfortable (see page 132).

Mounting from a block, or a handy rock or bank if you are out hacking, will reduce the strain on your horse's back. It is also a good idea to give his back a break from your weight from time to time, so dismount and walk or rest your horse for a while if you have been riding for a couple of hours.

A horse that is braced and moves stiffly, and does not move straight or lift his back, will generally have more problems with pressure and rubbing from saddles, so learn to train your horse as well as possible (see pages 144–147 and 165–167).

Treeless saddles

Most 'treeless' saddles actually include some hard parts, so may be better described as 'part-treed'. They have been developed in response to problems caused by ill-fitting treed saddles. Contrary to popular belief, these saddles still have to be fitted to the horse to some degree – they are not 'one size/shape fits all', although the same saddle can usually be adapted relatively easily to fit a number of horses.

Advantages
• Most parts of the saddle move with the horse, so with good designs there is less danger of causing pressure points than with a treed saddle.
• The horse's shoulders are often freed up.
• There is minimal danger of the saddle 'bridging' (see page 82).
• The rider is closer to the horse in many designs and can feel his movement better.
• The saddle will usually continue to fit the horse even when he changes shape.

Disadvantages
• The rider's weight is not spread as well as with a treed saddle, so a heavy rider or many hours in the saddle may cause seatbone or stirrup-bar pressure points.
• The saddle moves with the horse, so the effects of poor riding may be magnified.
• Some designs do not provide spine clearance.
• Some designs may create pressure at the withers/shoulders or cantle if there are hard parts in these areas.

Does my horse have a saddle fit problem?

It is relatively easy to check if your horse's movement is being restricted by his saddle.

1) Lunge or work your horse loose without his saddle and note how he moves (a video camera is useful here).
2) Do the same with him wearing his saddle and then compare his movement.
3) Now ride him and again compare his movement.

Do all this on both reins, and in walk, trot and canter – some problems only show up in faster gaits.

Rubbing, the appearance of white hairs on the withers or spine, lumps beneath the skin and so on are also signs that there is a problem with the fit of your saddle.

Poor saddle fit can eventually cause major physical problems in your horse, so it makes sense and is kinder to him to get your saddle checked by a reputable saddle fitter if you have even the slightest suspicion that it does not fit your horse well.

A number of behaviour and training problems may actually be due to poor saddle fit, including:
• Biting or moving away when being saddled.
• Moving away when you try to mount.
• Napping.
• Bucking, especially when going into canter (see page 168).
• Reluctance to move into faster gaits.
• Jogging (especially downhill).
• Difficulties working on one rein (the saddle may be asymmetrical).
• Refusal to jump (see page 170).

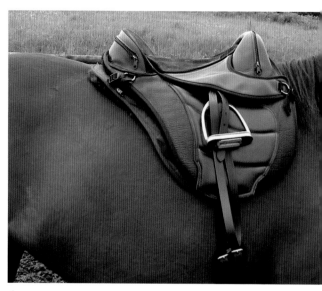

△ **This version of a treeless saddle has rigid parts in the pommel and cantle but is otherwise soft and flexible.**

Saddling difficulties

If your horse has had problems with poor saddle fit, he may have developed objections to being saddled that do not simply disappear when he is fitted with a better saddle. This is 'remembered pain' and your horse will probably need to experience a good number of pain-free saddlings before he will forget about it and accept the process happily. To help him resolve this issue (and you to get the saddle on him!) you can use approach-and-retreat (see page 67) to show him that moving away, nipping or cow-kicking are not successful strategies and that the saddle no longer hurts.

Your horse may also object to being saddled because he finds being ridden a confusing and unpleasant experience, so learn to train and ride your horse as well as you can (see Chapter 4).

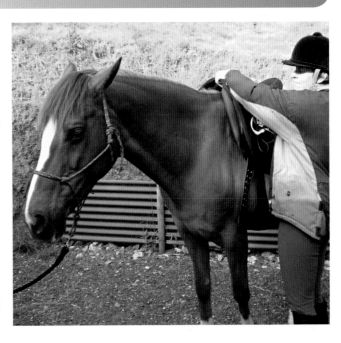

▷ **This mare has had major problems with ill-fitting saddles in the past. Although her new saddle fits well, she is still a little wary as the handler places it in position and may continue to be so for some time to come.**

△ **Soft and flexible at the pommel to avoid any pinching, this saddle has a part-tree to support the rider and spread the weight.**

△ **This treed saddle is modular, offering a range of interchangeable and adjustable options that allow it to be adapted for a range of horses, riders and activities. Innovations such as this now appear regularly on the market, making it easier than ever to find a saddle to suit horses that previously would have been difficult to fit.**

3 FACE TO FACE WITH YOUR HORSE

Whenever you handle your horse, you are also training him – whether you intend to or not! It is therefore a good idea to build an understanding of how the human–horse interaction works, the signals you may unwittingly be sending to your horse and how to teach him from the ground what you *do* want him to know rather than what you *don't*.

WHY GROUNDWORK?

Most of us are familiar with groundwork techniques such as lungeing and long-lining, which are widely used to prepare young horses for riding. Ideas and cues that the horse will need later are introduced without the added encumbrance of a rider, so that when the rider does eventually get on him the horse has at least a basic grasp of what is required. Older horses can also benefit from this type of work, to help them learn how best to carry themselves and to master the rudiments of some of the more advanced manoeuvres before the rider gets on.

Building a relationship

One use of groundwork is to teach the horse what we need him to know when we ride. At the same time, whether we are aware of it or not, we are also setting the ground rules of our relationship with the horse.

When you are lungeing or long-lining your horse, for example, you are communicating with him deliberately through cues. You are also communicating with him – consciously or unconsciously – through your body language, focus, intent and energy, as well as the attitude you bring to the work (see 'Your attitude', right). The horse is exceptionally good at reading these kinds of communications (see pages 42–43 and 97), and it is through this as much as the actual work you do with him that your relationship will develop.

It therefore makes sense to gain some understanding of how all this works and how best to use both the obvious and less obvious ways of communicating with your horse, so that you can build the relationship you want with him rather than the one you don't.

Your attitude

We all bring a certain attitude to working with horses, which may change from day to day or even moment to moment. For example, you may be:

- **Confident** that you can do the job and that somehow everything will work out well, even if you have never tried this particular technique before.
- **Fearful** of the horse, of making a mistake, or of failing to achieve what you had hoped.
- **Uncertain** of both your technical expertise and your ability to take charge of the interaction with your horse.
- **Angry** at something else going on in your life and, by default, with your horse for not responding as you feel he should.

The list goes on, but whatever your attitude at a particular time, you can rest assured that your horse will know and react accordingly. It therefore pays to recognize the attitude you bring to your horse and work consciously to make it as positive as you can.

Helping *you* learn

Working with your horse on the ground not only benefits him – it is also easier for *you* to learn how to communicate with him and start building your relationship while your feet are still on terra firma.

◁ **Walking through open fields and woods she has never been in before, with no other horses around, this mare is calm and relaxed as she has learned to rely on her handler in any and every situation. Previously, she was not easy to handle or ride, and had a tendency to rear when she felt under stress. The new relationship between horse and handler has been built over time through good groundwork.**

Dry land is our 'natural habitat': we don't generally need to pay attention to staying upright or walking along, which means we are free to pay attention to the horse. You can learn to 'read' the horse, practise techniques and principles, and achieve the results you want, without the added challenge of sitting on a moving animal and trying to *feel* what is happening (which does not necessarily come naturally) rather than *see* it (which does).

△ **This mare understands the groundwork she has learned in the arena and lunges quietly in an open field. From groundwork like this...**

△ **...come performances like this. This mare competes successfully at endurance, dressage and showjumping.**

Everyday 'groundwork'

Groundwork doesn't take place only in the arena on a lunge or long lines. Whenever you catch your horse in the field, lead him from A to B, groom him, tack him up, muck out his stable, adjust his rugs, load him in the trailer and the 101 other things you do with and around him every day, you are training your horse from the ground and building your relationship with him, for better or worse. You therefore need to be aware of how you present yourself to your horse and the way in which you handle him, all the time you are with him.

However, if you get things wrong, lose concentration or respond to your horse's actions in a way that is counterproductive (and we all do), don't despair. Instead, try to use the experience positively, as feedback to help you do better next time (and even better the time after that).

TAKE A LOOK AT YOUR HORSE

All horses are the same – but different! In other words, everything covered in Chapter 1 is true of all horses, but their temperaments and personalities vary. It is important to take this into account when you start working with your horse.

How reactive is he?

Horses naturally want to be comfortable physically, mentally and emotionally, and when they experience 'pressure' of any kind they will adjust – usually, but not always, by moving – to try to regain the feeling of being at ease (see page 30). All horses are the same in this respect.

However, where they differ is in the intensity of their responses to stimuli and, to some degree, in what those responses may be. For example, imagine you are lungeing a horse that has never worked this way before. You begin by asking him simply to move from halt to walk with, say, a click of your tongue and a flick of the lunge line:

• Horse 1 may react by shooting forward in canter and then, once he has reached the end of the lunge line, turn to face the 'danger'.
• Horse 2 does not appear to notice that anything has happened at all and remains rooted to the spot.
• Horse 3 moves off quietly in walk.

In this one moment, each of the three horses has demonstrated something about his natural level of reactivity. It is then up to you, the trainer, to work from here to bring horses 1 and 2 to the point where they respond in the same way as horse 3. This will involve adjusting your cues as you go and 'reading' the horse at every stage, until you achieve the result you want (see pages 95–99).

You can help your horse to change

So, training needs to be adjusted to take account of each horse's natural reactions in order to arrive at the same result. This does not mean making allowances for your horse to the point where you lose sight of your training goals. He may have certain tendencies, but his reactions are not fixed and can be moulded and trained to create the horse you want, within his natural limitations.

This opens the way to turning apparently negative character traits into positive ones (always bearing in mind that what is 'negative' to one person may be 'positive' to another!). For example:
• A slow cob that appears immune to almost anything that happens around him and largely ignores his rider's exhortations to move out of a walk, may have started life with a naturally low level of reactivity. However, whatever responsiveness he did possess has successfully been schooled out of him by poor training and riding. We know it's still in there – he can gallop around the field with the rest of the herd when he's sufficiently motivated – and with skill, time and commitment it can be schooled back in (see pages 156–159). We then have a responsive horse that is also 'bombproof'.
• The cob may never be a world beater – yet neither will the performance horse with superb movement and ability but with a tendency to be super-reactive to both his rider and his surroundings. However, train this horse with the emphasis on getting his mind right rather than pushing him through his performances regardless, and you may have that world beater.

△ **Arabians have a reputation for being reactive, but this purebred is happy to stand while the streamers are waved all around him.**

Assessing your horse

Unless you are setting out to buy the horse of your dreams – in which case, it makes sense to find one with the natural level of responsiveness (and physical attributes) you need – it is a good idea to check where your horse lies on a notional 'scale of reactivity'. Working him on a lunge line or loose in a safe enclosure (see pages 113–117 and 122–124) is a good way to judge his responses. Unless he is a virtually untouched youngster, some of these will demonstrate his natural level of reactivity, others will show you what he has learned so far about the human–horse interaction (see page 98). As you ask him to walk, trot, stop and turn, for example, are his responses:
• Slow and sluggish?
• Swift yet calm?
• Bordering on fleeing, and out of all proportion to your cues?
And so on. Your training can then be adjusted accordingly.

Assessing yourself

Once you have taken a look at your horse's tendencies, it is a good idea to take a look at your own. Are you naturally:
• Calm and assured?
• Timid and anxious?
• Forceful and aggressive?
• Erratic and emotional?
And so on. It is, of course, possible to make a conscious effort over time to change your natural tendencies – just like the horse, your reactions are not necessarily set in stone and certain character traits (including the last three listed above) are definitely counterproductive in working with any horse.

However, it is also true that some human character types will find it easier to work with some equines than others. For example:
• If you have a lot of energy and a strong personality, you should find it easy to motivate a more laid-back horse but may send a more sensitive type into orbit.
• If you are more introverted and find it difficult to project much power, a more phlegmatic horse may ignore you but you might get on well with a reactive character that needs quiet handling.

The full spectrum

If you want to become really good at training and riding horses, ultimately you will need to learn to move instantly from one end of the spectrum to other, as the situation dictates: at one moment powerful and decisive, the next soft and releasing – and any point in between (see pages 95–102).

You can learn a lot by working through your difficulties with a horse that might not suit your temperament as well as another, but sometimes it is better to be realistic. If you are looking for a horse to buy, or are really struggling with the one you have, it may make sense to seek out a new equine partner whose natural tendencies will make the training process easier on you both.

ATTENTION AND CALMNESS

Before you ask your horse to do anything, you need his attention. This may sound obvious, but horses can actually perform many of the actions you want – after a fashion – without being 'with you' mentally. Check this out next time you are at a show or other event: you may be surprised at how many horses are simply going through the motions, while mentally they are back at the lorry, fleeing from the noisy fairground rides or taking comfort from their friends in the warm-up ring.

Attention and safety

If your only concern is that your horse does what you want when you want him to, the fact that mentally he is somewhere else may not matter too much – until it does. When events begin to go a little pear-shaped, the horse will tend to go where his attention is, and most of us would prefer that to mean that he stays with us.

Like us, horses get good at what they practise, and if your horse practises ignoring you most of the time (even if he appears to be 'performing'), that's exactly what he will do when the going gets tough. On the other hand, if he practises listening to and taking direction from you, that's what he'll do when you find yourselves in a difficult situation. Getting your horse's attention on you rather than elsewhere is therefore an important prerequisite to your both staying safe.

Quality control

If you are concerned not only about your horse responding to you but also about the way in which he responds, getting his attention is an essential starting point.

For your horse to respond instantly and smoothly to your cues, he first needs to be paying attention to you. If he is not, he won't necessarily be aware that you have asked him to do something, so there is little hope of him responding promptly. It is unfair to blame the horse for not answering your request if you did not set him up to be able to hear it.

If your horse's attention is elsewhere, looking out for dangers or wondering where his friends are, the chances are that he will also be tense and braced in his mouth, neck and body. From here, it is impossible for him to respond softly and easily to your cues, and this is when many people resort to forceful tactics in an attempt to get the horse to perform. At that point, it may appear that there is no alternative.

Look at the situation a little differently, however, and you may find that there is another way through. Make getting your horse's attention your first priority, and start working on some of the other aspects described in this chapter and in Chapter 4, and you will discover that good quality performance follows as a result. Attending to your horse's mental state should therefore be your first concern; performance should be your last.

This young mare's attention is scattered, rather than focused on her handler and the work they are doing. She is moving along as asked but very crookedly – her focus is somewhere else and her feet would like to go there. Her right ear (barely) acknowledges the handler, but her eyes are riveted on what is going on further up the arena.

A little later in the session and the picture is totally different. The horse is working with relaxed concentration and her focus is on the job in hand.

Where is *your* attention?

If you want your horse to give his attention to you, you have to give your attention to your horse – all the time you are with him.

This doesn't necessarily mean focusing intently on him to the exclusion of all else. It does mean 'being there' mentally, aware of your horse and ready to give him help and direction when he needs it – not 'wandering off' to think about how you and your horse look to anyone who might be watching, or whether you are going to be late for your next appointment, or how you hope you won't get stuck in traffic on the way home.

Next time you are with your horse, keep a check on where you are mentally – you may be surprised at how often you 'leave' the situation. If your horse then leaves too, you can hardly blame him. Practise bringing yourself back each time you notice you have left: you may find this quite tiring at first, but eventually it will become second nature.

Where is your horse's attention?

A horse's attention is naturally scattered: he needs to be able to check constantly on everything that is going on around him in order to feel safe. His eyes and ears will flick first in one direction, then another. Their independent movement (see pages 8–15) allows the horse to focus on more than one place at a time.

Checking on the position of your horse's ears and the focus of his eyes will allow you to monitor where his attention is moment by moment. If he gets as far as moving his head and neck in a particular direction and staring fixedly at that point with his ears sharply pricked, you will be left in no doubt.

Bringing him back to you

When you begin interacting with your horse, you will be asking him to concentrate his attention mainly on one point: you. This runs directly counter to his natural inclination, but at the same time it is in his (and your) best interests if he is to function happily and safely in the human world.

Checking where your horse's attention is and when necessary bringing it back to you is something you should be doing whenever you are with your horse. This does not mean that he has to be rigidly focused on you alone for every second you are together: remember that a horse can happily pay attention to more than one thing at a time. You will need to learn to tell the difference between:

1 A horse that is focused on you to the exclusion of all else.
2 A horse that is with you mentally, but is also quietly checking out other aspects of his surroundings.
3 A horse that has become so distracted that mentally he has left you altogether.

In some situations, you may need horse 1; mostly, horse 2 will do fine. If he starts to leave, and before you find yourself with horse 3 on your hands, you need to take action to get his attention back with you.

What you actually do to regain your horse's attention is not as important as your timing: if you can catch your horse's first thought of leaving (a twitch of an ear, glance of an eye, tightening of a muscle), it will be easier to get him back than if you wait until he has decided he needs to leave physically as well!

1) The handler is looking and heading one way, while the horse has been distracted and is looking in another direction entirely.
2) The rope has tightened but the horse persists in looking off to the right – and the handler's head begins to turn...
3) ...until she is looking the same way that he is! This is a good example of the *horse* deciding where the horse–human partnership should be focusing.

There are suggestions of ways to get your horse's attention in various situations – leading, lungeing, long-lining, loose work – in the relevant sections of this chapter.

This mare begins to focus on the horses in the paddock to her right, while the handler continues to focus straight ahead. Both are still walking directly towards the photographer.

A few strides later, however, and the horse's legs have followed the line of her attention and she is heading off to the right, away from the handler – who should have acted while all this was still just a thought in the horse's mind.

About control

Once you can get your horse's attention and bring it back easily when it strays *before* he leaves completely, you will begin to eliminate the need for heavy corrections, 'discipline' and fighting with your horse. In other words, if you can get your horse with you *mentally*, you will not have to resort to using force to control him *physically*.

An exercise in attention

If you want to check your horse's powers of concentration and help him learn to focus more on you than on outside influences, this exercise can be useful. You will need your horse in a headcollar with a long lead rope or lunge line attached.

• Stand in front of your horse and a few metres away, with slack in the rope.

• Ask for his attention by gently jiggling the lead rope, flicking your fingers, slapping your leg or whatever else you think will work. Start with a small movement or noise, and if necessary (but only if necessary) build up to whatever it takes to get your horse to focus on you. For some horses, this may mean jumping up and down on the spot and waving your arms; others may respond to as little as a twitch of your finger.

• As soon as your horse gives you his attention, stop whatever you were doing and stand relaxed, still and quiet, with your focus on him. See how long it takes before his attention wanders – you may be surprised how even a second or two is more than many horses can manage.

• Each time your horse 'leaves' you, ask for his attention again, always starting with a small request and only building up to something bigger if necessary.

• Set yourself a target of, say, three seconds and at that point go to your horse and pet him.

• When your horse can give you his attention for three seconds with relative ease, finish the exercise.

• Repeat this over a few days, gradually building up the time for which you ask for your horse's attention: around eight to ten seconds is a good target. See how small you can make your requests and still get a response.

Because you remove all 'pressure' – the jiggling rope, flicking fingers, waving arms or whatever else you are using – as soon as the horse gives you his attention, you are showing him that there is a positive benefit for him in doing so. When he 'leaves', things become a little noisy and uncomfortable; when he stays with you, everything is quiet and easy.

This horse is distracted by his fieldmate grazing in the paddock in the background, and the handler is raising her hand to ask him with the rope to bring his attention back to her.

The horse is paying attention to the handler once again, but the position of his ears indicates that he is still well aware of what is going on around him.

Building calmness and trust

When your horse begins paying attention to you, he will automatically start to become calm. This is no surprise: a horse that is distracted by every little occurrence around him will be tense and anxious and will find it very difficult to relax.

Once your horse is calm, *then* you can start to work with him without him 'fleeing'. This also signals the first steps in building trust, in that your horse realizes he can safely forget about looking out for dangers while he is working with you. You are beginning to become more important to him than other factors.

△ Calm and attentive: this horse bends softly around the circle and does not pull on the lunge line, her neck is relaxed and head low, her eyes are soft, and her ears are floppy but aware of both the surroundings and the handler as she waits for her next instruction. This is the state of mind in which horses can learn.

STARTING WORK

How do you teach a horse something? In fact, it's better if you don't. It's actually much easier to set up the situation and let the horse learn for himself. Then he will be committed to the choices he has made.

Taking responsibility

Your first responsibility as your horse's 'teacher' is to assume nothing. As we saw in Chapter 1, the horse is a horse and his behaviour, motivations and view of the world around him are quite different to ours. Making human assumptions about the horse's understanding and motives when he reacts to our demands can have unfortunate consequences:

• On the one hand, we label the horse 'stupid' when he does not respond as we think he should.

• On the other, we assign him human motives such as malice, a sense of humour or the desire to make us look foolish.

Neither tends to have a good outcome for the horse. Instead of leaping to conclusions, perhaps we should add a simple question to each of the above sentences: 'But have we made it clear to him what we want?'

The truth is that the horse is just a horse, behaving as a horse does, and it is *our* responsibility to show him the rules of behaviour when he is with people, how to cope with an alien (human) environment and how he should respond to alien (human) demands.

Pressure and release

For a horse, 'pressure' comes in many guises and may be physical, mental or emotional. It might involve, for example, the lightest touch of a human hand, or the sound of a voice, or the powerful intent of another horse moving towards him, or the fear of being isolated from his friends, or anything in between.

When a horse feels himself under pressure, he will adjust (usually by moving) until he feels at ease once again (see pages 30 and 89): this is his 'release'. Because horses naturally move away from pressure of any kind and actively search for a release, they are actually very easy to train – *if* we apply this principle consistently, in ways they can understand.

Consistency

It almost doesn't matter what method you use to train your horse, as long as you apply it consistently. Horses hate grey areas; black and white, yes and no are much more to their liking.

If you are constantly moving the goal posts for your horse, he will find it very difficult to learn what you are trying to teach (in fact, he may actually learn something else entirely) and he will quickly become confused. He may then, for example:

• Offer erratic responses in a desperate attempt to discover what you want.

• Stop trying to find the answers to your training 'questions'.

• Attempt to leave the training situation, physically (which can be dangerous) or mentally (he 'shuts down').

Being consistent is therefore of utmost importance when you are working with your horse.

Rewarding the try

When you are helping your horse to learn something new, it is essential that as soon as he offers a response that is even roughly what you want, you reward his attempt immediately. Your horse learns from the *release* (not from the pressure).

Once the basic response is in place, you can then shape it however you want. Consider the following example. You touch your horse on his hindquarters to ask him to move them away from you – your horse leans his hindquarters into your hand, putting more pressure on himself. Your hand remains in place. Your horse next tries lifting the hind leg nearest to you and placing it down close to his other hind leg – you release the pressure of your hand to reward him for this try. From here, you can shape his response by waiting for more movement each time before releasing your hand pressure, until eventually the horse steps his hindquarters away from you.

Learning to recognize your horse's try, reward it and then build on this is effective because it is readily understood by the horse. Expecting perfection at the first attempt and then correcting everything wrong with it – or even punishing the horse – is not.

Timing and feel

Closely linked to the idea of rewarding your horse's try are the concepts of timing and feel.

• One of the best ways to create a responsive, motivated horse is to release your cues as early as you possibly can: in other words, the *timing* of your release is crucial.

• In order to get your timing right, you need to be able to *feel* when your horse is about to respond, or is even thinking about responding, so that you can release early.

Timing and feel can be learned, and a good instructor will be able to help you with this. You first need to give your horse your attention, so that you will be aware of the shift of weight, softening of a muscle or change in feel in the lead rope that signals he is about to make a move. Then you need to practise – whenever you are with your horse.

Training as experiment

There are a number of different methods for training horses successfully. Rather than viewing training as the application of particular techniques to achieve particular results, it can be more helpful to see it as the application of principles – such as those outlined on page 95 – and each training task as something of an experiment.

After all, when you first offer a cue to your horse you do not know what he is going to do in response, and if what he offers does not appear in the textbook, you may rapidly reach the limits of a specific technique. This is often the point at which crude emotion and brute force take over. Remember: there is always more than one way to accomplish a task.

In order to develop flexibility and effectiveness in training, you need to get feedback from your horse to help you decide how to proceed. You may need to make use of any or all of the following at different times:

• **Waiting for a response** Apply a cue and then give your horse time to respond – he needs to think, organize his body and then

1) This horse begins by leaning into the light pressure applied to his headcollar to ask him to step back. He is also distracted and turning his head away, not focusing on the job at hand.

2) To gain his attention, the handler applies more pressure and the horse reacts by flinging his head up, looking for a release. The handler keeps the pressure on the rope, so as not to reward the horse for a response she does not want.

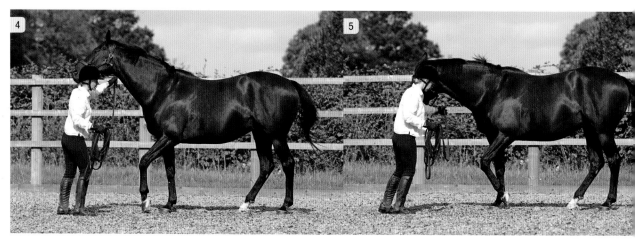

4) The horse takes a step back but again pushes his head up and braces his neck against the pressure, which remains constant.

5) Finally, he lowers his head, softens his neck a little and steps back. This is the moment to release.

move. If instead you increase the pressure or apply your cue again immediately, you may miss the chance to reward your horse's try. Once your horse understands what is being asked, you can expect an increasingly prompt response.

• **Increasing the pressure** If your horse does not respond at all, one option is to increase the pressure of the initial cue until he does. Always offer the lightest cue first: the one you would eventually like him to respond to. Bear in mind that for each horse in each moment there is a degree of pressure that is so light he will ignore or not even notice it, and a degree that is so heavy he will resist it; somewhere in between is a pressure that is just enough for him to notice and feel motivated enough to do

something about. Once your horse understands what you want, you can reduce the pressure until he is responding to the lightest possible cue.

• **Introducing a secondary cue** If your horse does not respond to your initial cue, he may need you to clarify what you are asking by introducing another one. In the previous example, if your horse does not respond to hand pressure on his hindquarters, possible secondary cues might include swinging the end of the lead rope in your free hand towards his back end, bringing his head around towards you using the lead rope, or stepping towards his hindquarters with energy and intent. You need to find something that will motivate your horse to respond. Apply your primary cue, then if he doesn't respond use your secondary cue until he does. Once your horse understands what you want, you will be able to phase out your secondary cue.

Learning to learn

When you first apply a cue, your horse literally has to guess what it means. He will do this by trying out a variety of responses and searching for a release from the 'pressure' of the cue.

This is the point at which the dangers of assuming that the horse understands what you mean, just because you do, become most apparent. Even with an experienced horse, it is easy to think he knows what you want when in fact he doesn't. A good example is the horse that 'knows' a leg cue means 'go' but still has to be kicked every stride to keeping him moving (see pages 158–161).

3) With his head down, the horse leans heavily into the pressure and his feet are stuck. The handler steps towards him, to give him an idea of the direction in which she wants him to move.

▷ **The handler asks the horse to lead forward and he remains rooted to the spot. There are several possible interpretations of this situation, including:**

• **The horse knows what to do and is deliberately resisting (just to annoy the handler!) – but why would he do this, when it is easier to move?**

• **He does not understand that pressure on his head is a cue to move his feet, so reacts instinctively by bracing against the pull.**

• **He does not regard the handler as worth following, so makes his own decision about whether or not to move (see pages 100–102).**

When your horse responds to your cue in ways other than the one you want, it is all too easy to assume he is being 'resistant' or 'naughty' and react accordingly (see page 95). If instead you see this as him simply searching for the answer to your question, all you have to do is wait until he hits upon the response you want and then release your cue.

At this point, your horse may have tried many responses and may not actually know what he did to get your release! On subsequent repetitions, he will rapidly begin to eliminate some options and narrow these down to the ones he gave just before you released the cue. Eventually, he will understand that it was the last response he gave that earned the release. As horses progress in their training, they come to realize that it is always this last response that is the one you want, and will begin learning new cues in just one or two trials.

It should now be obvious how crucial it is that you always release your cue on the response you want and never on one you don't.

Providing choices
You cannot make a horse learn something. You might be able to make him *do* something, but he won't have *learned* anything – except perhaps that the two of you are in an adversarial relationship.

You need to set up the situation so that you give your horse a choice and he then teaches himself what you want him to learn because it is the easiest option. Think about the example of asking your horse to move his hindquarters. You didn't make him do it by using fear and physical force: you provided a motivation (light hand pressure, and perhaps a secondary cue, on one side of his hindquarters) for him to make the choice you wanted and then rewarded him instantly when he did. When the horse discovers this, and that your response to his choice is absolutely consistent, he will be committed to this course of action and offer to repeat it every time you give him the cue.

Rewarding himself

In many instances, you can set up training situations so that when the horse gives the response you want, he releases *himself*, so you need do nothing. For example, if you put light pressure on the lead rope to ask your horse to step towards you, as soon as he does so the rope will go slack and give him his release (see page 102). If you are worried about your timing, feel or level of expertise, this is ideal!

Learned behaviours
Unless you are starting with an untouched horse (and, if you have the skill, these can be the easiest of all to train), your horse will already have learned a certain amount about people and what they want him to do – some you want him to know and some you wish he didn't.

Because horses set up patterns of behaviour quickly and easily, this makes them easy to train but much more difficult to retrain. It is therefore doubly important that when you set out to teach your horse something, you make absolutely sure *that* is what he actually learns. Again, be aware that whenever you are with your horse, you are training him (see box on page 89).

What's in it for the horse?
If your horse is to enjoy learning from and working with you, there has to be something in it for him.
• Horses naturally understand pressure and release (see page 95), so as long as the timing of your releases is consistent and logical to the horse, this will be his first and also his most important reward.
• You can add to this by stroking or a good wither scratch if you like (horses do not generally like enthusiastic patting), and most come to enjoy this, but its importance to the horse is a distant second to that of a well-timed release.
• Despite what many people appear to believe, most horses are not naturally lazy and work-shy (but may quickly become so if subjected to inconsistent and confusing training – see page 95).

△ **A pleasant scratch can be a good extra reward for a horse – and this one is clearly enjoying the moment – but should not take the place of a well-timed release, which is far more meaningful to the horse.**

They appear to enjoy the feeling of free, balanced movement, and if through training we can help them to carry themselves well under a rider, this constitutes a reward in itself.

• Getting your horse's attention, working on softness, and sorting out issues of personal space and who moves whom at the start of training (see pages 91–94, 100–102 and 109–112) will all help your horse become calm and mentally at ease. He will then be happy to work with you, simply because it makes him feel good.

Reading the horse

In order to train a horse well, you need to be able to 'read' him. This means, first, paying attention to him moment by moment (see page 92) and, second, learning to spot the signs that tell you he is tense or relaxed, focused or distracted, about to move or make a change to what he is already doing and so on. A good instructor will be able to help you with this.

When you can read your horse, you will be able to:
• Offer him a release as soon as he *thinks* about doing what you have asked.

• Decide when to reduce or increase the pressure of your cues, add another cue or simply wait for a response (see pages 96–97).
• Step in to help and direct him at the instant he needs you to do so.
• Recognize what he is going to do before he actually does it, enabling you to avoid the need for any kind of heavy corrections.

Intent, energy and focus

Whether or not you can read your horse, he can certainly read you (see pages 42–43). This means you can use your intent, energy and focus as cues, enabling your communication with your horse to become extremely subtle.

For example, you can flip the end of a lead rope at your horse's hindquarters with energy and intent, and he will move. Do the same action with softer movements and little energy, and (assuming he has already learned that ropes are not out to get him) he will remain still. The fact that your horse makes these kinds of distinctions easily opens up a whole range of training options.

1) The handler throws the rope over the mare's back in a relaxed manner with no intent to ask her to move. The mare can 'read' this and does not move her feet, but she is anxious so raises her head and turns it away.

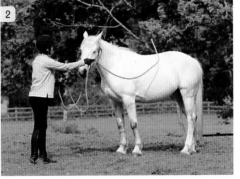

2) Next time she is less concerned, but still keeps an eye and ear on the moving rope.

3) The mare looks even more relaxed as the rope flips up against her shoulder and flank.

4) The handler flips the rope closer to the horse's head and she accepts this well, too.

5) Finally, the mare relaxes totally as the rope passes over and around her head.

SPACE AND MOVEMENT

Horses naturally understand about personal space and moving each other around – this is how they organize their relationships within the herd (see pages 44–47). Your job is to explain to your horse what his relationship with you (and other people) is to be by defining your personal space and moving him around – *not* the other way round!

The basis for your relationship

Because it is natural to him, your horse will accept the 'terms' you offer him without resentment. Most importantly, getting this right forms a solid basis for everything else you will ever do with your horse:

• He will understand and accept his role in your relationship, instead of constantly questioning who is in charge (and being obliged to take over whenever he finds that you are not). Remember: horses do not like grey areas (see page 95).

• He will be content for you to take the decisions for both of you. In a human world, horses' own decisions don't always follow health and safety guidelines!

• He will have peace of mind while he is in your company (since you will be doing most of the thinking), so will be happy to spend time working with you.

Bear in mind, too, that whatever you have (or have not) established about your relationship with your horse while you are on the ground will inevitably carry over into your ridden work.

A question of respect?

Many people regard a horse that pushes into his handler's space as 'rude' or 'disrespectful', but if he has never been shown the boundaries of that space in a consistent way, how can he possibly be expected to 'respect' them? This is your responsibility, not your horse's.

Defining your personal space

Before you can define your personal space for your horse, you need to decide what it is and then stick to it. This may sound obvious, but if you take a look you may find you are handling your horse in an inconsistent way without even realizing it: one moment allowing him to push up close, the next backing him off when he has trodden on your toe!

How big a space?

To be fair to your horse, the boundary of your personal space should be at least an arm's length (more if your horse is large and you are small). This way, he can see you easily and get some warning as to what you are going to ask him to do next. It will also enable you to use body language, focus and energy more effectively (see page 99), rather than always applying physical pressure to convey your requests.

Communicating boundaries to your horse

With some horses, using pressure on the lead rope to back them out to the boundary of your space every time they breach it can be enough to get your message across. However, this can take a large number of repetitions and many horses will continue to push into your space even then – a pattern of behaviour has been set up that they then think is correct. Generally, if what you are doing hasn't worked within, say, two or three repetitions, it probably isn't going to.

Much more effective is to use body language, intent and energy to define your boundaries. You will need a good instructor to help you with this in the beginning. With one horse, it may be enough to be (or act) confident, square your shoulders and perhaps take a small, sharp step towards him

◁ **If you have not shown your horse the boundaries of your space, the pleasant scratch on page 98 can quickly turn into him using you as nothing more than a convenient rubbing post! If you allow this, you cannot fairly expect the horse not to walk straight through you at other times.**

as he makes that first move into your space. With another, it may take everything you have to get him to back off, especially if he has had plenty of practice at backing *people* away from *him*!

Once the horse begins to get the idea, you will be able to reduce your signals, and quite soon he will stop trying to enter your space uninvited. Occasionally your horse may breach the boundary again, and it is important that you are absolutely consistent in redefining it – every time, wherever you are and whatever you are doing. It is unfair to your horse to do otherwise.

△ **This looks good: slack in the rope, the horse at a safe distance from the handler, and both standing motionless and relaxed**

Your space or his?

1) The horse has walked straight into the handler's space and begun rubbing his head on her.
2) The handler has stepped back to avoid the horse pushing on her, but this immediately tells him that he is the one directing movement, not her.
3) The handler squares up to the horse, using her raised arms and the lunge line to try to define her space and move him back out of it. Although he moves his head further away, his feet remain glued to the ground – the handler's actions are not 'big' enough to make an impression on this particular horse.
4) Finally, the handler decides to move the horse back out of her space using the lead rope. This gets the job done, but is unlikely to affect the horse's perception of her personal space in future.

Directing movement

Closely tied in with the issue of personal space is that of who directs movement, you or your horse? Most of the rest of this chapter is about ways of moving your horse around, starting with leading and moving on to lungeing, long-lining and loose work.

For now, the important point to remember is not to allow your horse to move you, unless your physical safety is under threat. It should always be you who moves your horse.

Good practice

Learning to define your personal space for your horse and then directing his movement can benefit your horsemanship in other ways, too:

• It is a good exercise in reading your horse (see page 99) and anticipating what he is about to do.

• You can practise doing as little as it takes to get a result, but also being committed if necessary to doing as much as it takes (and no more) to get a result.

• Your horse's reactions will tell you a lot about what he has already been taught (often inadvertently) by and about people.

Testing situations

There are many small, everyday ways (some of which you may not even notice) in which the horse tests personal space and who moves whom. If in doubt, he has to do this: he is not being 'mean', 'nasty' or 'pushy'. From his point of view, it is essential – for his survival – to know who is taking care of the decisions.

Some common everyday ways in which your horse might test the 'boundaries' include:

• Ignoring your request for him to move.
• Ignoring your request for him to stand still.
• Pushing you with his nose until you lean or step back.
• Stepping a shoulder towards you until you step away.
• Squashing you (even lightly!) against the stable wall.
• Swinging his hindquarters towards you in the stable, so that you then walk a curve around him to get to his head (effectively controlling your movement).
• Refusing to be caught in the field (very effectively controlling your movement).

By acting this way, your horse is asking you a question: 'Is it all right for me to do this?' If you allow him to continue the behaviour, you have effectively answered 'Yes.' This then tells your horse that he can and, indeed, needs to take charge in your relationship.

1) This handler approaches her horse with powerful intent and the mare immediately moves back. She is surprised by the 'volume' of the handler's actions and is a little tense and jerky in her movements, but the important thing at this first attempt is that the handler has been effective.

2) Next time, the handler is able to use less energy to get the desired response, and the horse is calmer and more relaxed as a result.

LEADING AND TYING

All domestic horses need to learn how to lead, as this is something that happens every time we do anything with them. Moreover, they need to learn to lead properly.

Many supposedly 'halter broken' horses actually aren't: much of the time, a horse like this will lead acceptably (although often it is difficult to tell who is taking whom for a walk), but when the going gets tough he may:

• Plant his feet and refuse to move.
• Barge past his handler and then drag them along.
• Pull away completely when frightened or excited.

A horse that acts is such ways has learned, through poor training, to make decisions that should actually be the handler's responsibility and may be putting both himself and his handler at risk.

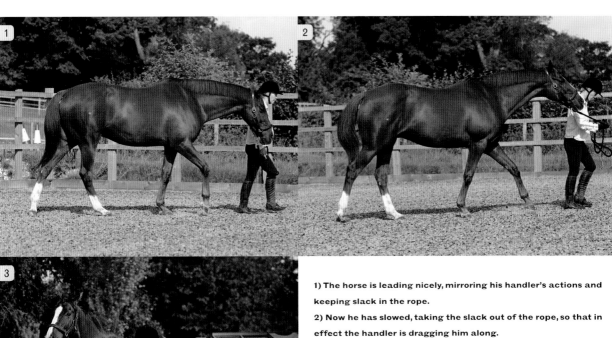

1) The horse is leading nicely, mirroring his handler's actions and keeping slack in the rope.

2) Now he has slowed, taking the slack out of the rope, so that in effect the handler is dragging him along.

3) This time the horse has quickened, so that he is pulling the handler along. These two extremes often occur in the same horse, since he – rather than the handler – is choosing the speed at which the two of them proceed, whether fast or slow.

What is good leading?

There are different ideas on the position the horse should adopt relative to the handler when being led, but as long as it's safe this probably isn't crucial. What is crucial is that the horse is with you mentally, following your lead, and understands that it's his job to keep the lead rope slack at all times and stay out of your personal space. He can only do this if he is calm and paying attention, and you are the same. Leading is such an everyday activity, it is easy to forget that every time you do it you are training your horse, for better or worse.

Staying out of your space

Your horse should already have learned to stay out of your personal space unless you invite him in (see pages 100–101). This is doubly important when you are on the move: it is very dangerous to lead a horse that may barge into or over you at any moment. Whenever you are leading your horse, make sure that he stays outside the boundary of your space at all times.

On the move

Once your horse is consistently giving to light pressure on the lead rope, it is time to get moving. He needs to learn to:

• Go when you go.
• Move at the speed you decide.
• Stop when you stop.

This is the beginning of the two of you working together, by synchronizing your movements (see page 45).

Your horse can learn to do this because he now understands that he should give to the rope rather than pull into it. Whenever he feels the beginnings of pressure on the rope – when you start to walk and he hesitates, if you walk faster or slower than he does, when you stop and he doesn't – he will look for a way to put the slack back into it.

Eventually, the rope will never tighten: as long as your horse is paying attention, he will adjust what he is doing to follow your lead and not allow the slack to be taken out of the rope.

Keeping the lead rope slack

For good leading, your horse needs to learn to give to light pressure on the lead rope, and you need to learn to release the pressure at the right time (see pages 95–96).

1) The handler has taken the slack out of the lead rope to ask the horse to move towards her, but he is paying her no attention and is therefore unlikely to think about moving his feet.
2) When the horse begins to take notice of the handler's request his feet start to move and slack appears in the rope, thereby rewarding himself – as long as the handler is careful not to take up the slack herself, but instead softens her fingers on the rope.
3) When he has halted, the handler steps towards him (not the other way round) to reward him with a rub.

◁ Even when you are holding the lead rope short, it is still possible to ensure it is slack whenever the horse is getting things right.

1) The handler is walking quickly, with long strides, and the mare is mirroring this almost exactly.

2) Her left ear shows she has noticed that something has changed as the handler slows and shortens her steps, and the mare's next step is slower and shorter too.

3) This photo taken from the other side of the horse shows that with a little more practice she is stepping in exactly the same way as the handler.

Making turns

There are obviously two directions in which you can turn – left or right – and these present two different situations to the horse. If you are leading the horse from his left (near) side:

• When you make a turn to the left, if the horse does not follow you, the rope will tighten. With everything he has understood already, he should learn to make this turn quite easily.

• When you make a turn to the right, the rope does not tighten and you will be stepping towards the horse rather than away from him. If he really has learned to stay out of your space whatever the situation (see pages 100–101), he should step away and around the turn in order to maintain the distance between you.

1) The handler is turning left, but the horse is distracted and is still walking straight ahead. As the handler turns further to the left, the rope begins to tighten…

2) …and the horse feels it, so she begins to swing her head and neck to the left and make the turn in order to put slack back into the rope.

3) Now horse and handler are operating more as one unit to complete the turn.

1) The handler begins to turn right, but the horse ignores this and continues walking straight ahead.

2) Now the horse begins to feel the 'pressure' of the handler's position and she starts to turn.

3) Horse and handler complete the turn together. At no point did the handler need to touch the horse or take the slack out of the rope.

Keeping your horse's attention

It can be dangerous to lead a horse that is easily distracted and then forgets you are on the end of the rope. It is natural and acceptable for your horse to look briefly at events going on in the world around him, but if he begins to tense up and stare fixedly in one direction, you need to get his attention back with you – preferably well before his thought turns into action. To do this, you might, for example:

• Make a small noise.
• Change speed or direction.
• Jiggle the lead rope or put a little pressure on it.

If you find yourself having to do something big, such as yanking your horse's head back to you, you acted too late. The key is to catch your horse's thought to 'leave' as early as possible. Your action can then be small, and you will be directing your horse rather than correcting him.

Why change the habit of a lifetime?

Some horses have spent a great deal of their lives pulling on lead ropes and knocking people over. They have continued to do so because each time it has led to a benefit for them, for example:

• The handler puts slack in the rope when the horse pulls.
• The horse can go where he wants to go (or not go where he doesn't want to go), and the handler has not managed to prevent him from doing so.
• The horse can barge through and pull away from his handler whenever he wants to leave the situation – often this means he returns to his friends in the stables or field, which constitutes a huge reward.

It can therefore be difficult to change the horse's behaviour pattern once it is established. If your horse is in this category, you may need expert help if you are to stay safe *and* convince him that there is an easier and more beneficial way of doing things.

1) Horse and handler are both heading left, but the horse has been distracted and this has drawn the handler's attention away from the task at hand…

2) …to the point where she has allowed slack into the rope, thereby rewarding the horse for his inattention. She slows down…

3) …and both of them come almost to a halt. The horse, rather than the handler, has set the agenda.

4) Things are going better here, although the handler is looking back at the horse which may cause him to wonder where they are headed and whether he should be making the decision over direction!

5) Horse and handler are now functioning better as a team, focusing on where they are going, and look a lot more relaxed.

Tying up

You should teach your horse to tie up after he has learned to lead and is consistently working to keep slack in the rope: this is what he needs to know in order not to pull back when tied.

When you first tie up your horse, check that when he feels pressure on the rope he steps forward or to the side, not back, in order to release it. You can hold the end of the rope in your hand to start with, rather than tying it, while you make sure that your horse responds correctly each time he feels the rope. Make sure that you do not take the slack out of the rope when he releases himself from the pressure.

1) The rope is threaded through a tie ring and the handler holds the loose end, with the rope slack.

2) The horse is distracted and raises her head, putting some tension on the rope. The handler does nothing – she neither pulls on the rope nor feeds slack into it – so the horse receives the same feel as if she were tied directly to the ring.

3) The horse has felt the tension in the rope and moved forward to relieve herself of the pressure – again, the handler has done nothing. This is the result you need from the horse, consistently, before tying her directly to the ring.

Safety first

Retraining a horse that consistently pulls back when tied can be dangerous and is definitely a job for an expert.

1) This horse is clearly distracted and restless, moving his feet around instead of standing still. His head may be tied, but his mind is elsewhere.

2) Another horse is led by just out of shot and he immediately focuses all his attention on it…

3) …then a moment later he translates this into action, pulling back hard and breaking the tie, so that he can set off to join his friend. This constitutes a huge 'reward' for a horse, and he will be very likely to repeat the behaviour.

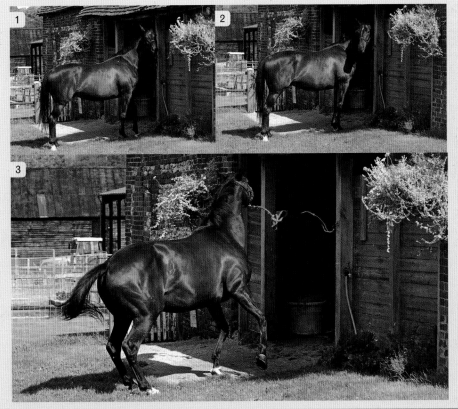

Ground tying

Teaching your horse to ground tie will help you learn how to teach your horse something very specific, and of course it's extremely handy to have a horse that will remain standing exactly where you have left him without having to be tied up. All it takes is the feel of the rope dropping to the ground and he will remain rooted to the spot until you return to collect him.

1) To begin teaching the horse to ground tie, the handler allows the lunge line to drop to the ground, while keeping the coils safely in her hand. The feel of the line hitting the ground will become the horse's cue to stand still, just as the handler is doing here. If the horse moves, the handler will return him to his place, preferably by using body language to create some 'pressure' while he is moving, and releasing (by standing still) when he stops.

2) Once the horse can stand still with the handler close by, she can move further away from him, returning to reward him with a rub whenever he stands still for the required length of time. This should be built up slowly. Gradually, the handler repeats the process at greater distances from the horse.

3) The next stage is for the handler to drop the line entirely, and if the previous training has been effective the horse will take this as his cue to stand still, even though they are no longer physically connected through the line.

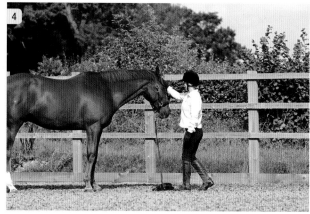

4) Each time the horse is successful, the handler returns to him and rewards him with a rub and a break from the exercise.

WORKING ON SOFTNESS

Not only do you want your horse to respond to pressure of any kind by giving to it, you want him to do this softly – without fear, tension or bracing. From this perspective, it's more important *how* your horse does something than *that* he does it (see page 91).

A horse can respond quickly and lightly, and give the impression of being well trained, but still be extremely tight physically, both mentally and emotionally. Such a horse is certainly moving away from pressure but is not seeking or moving into softness.

The soft horse

A horse that is totally soft is at your disposal. He is:
• Relaxed and happy to do his work.
• Waiting for your next instruction.
• Responsive to the lightest cues.
• Unconcerned about what is going on around him, or where other horses might be.
• Completely 'with you' mentally.

The above is the ideal and is something we can all aim for with our horses.

Physically, the soft horse uses only the muscles he needs to do the job at hand most efficiently, and no more. For the ridden horse, there are huge benefits:
• He has 'turned off' all the muscles of his topline, from his jaw to his tail.
• This allows the muscles of his underline to 'switch on' and do the work instead.
• Only from here is genuine collection possible (see page 165).

1) At first glance this horse looks as though he is working relatively well on the lunge, but on closer inspection we can see his movement is neither fluid nor really going forward.

2) As soon as he is asked for a little more effort – and the handler has got her lunge line in a tangle as she tries hard to urge him on – he pokes his nose, pulls on the line and swishes his tail, confirming suspicions that he was not really putting himself at the handler's disposal in the first place.

Why do horses brace themselves?

The short answer is – we teach them to. Physically, the horse feels he needs to protect himself by bracing his muscles because we:
• Push and pull him around.
• Use heavy cues.
• Mis-time the release of pressure, or give no release at all.
• Offer no softness ourselves.

Mentally and emotionally, the horse becomes tense and anxious because we:
• Handle him inconsistently.
• Do not take charge of decision-making.
• Allow emotions to take over.
• Offer no softness ourselves.
It doesn't have to be this way.

△ This Icelandic horse is working softly on the lunge. She is relaxed and attentive, her topline is released and rounded, she is bending softly around the circle and is keeping slack in the line at all times.

The braced horse

If your horse is braced physically, he will also be braced mentally (and vice versa). If this is the case, in everything he does he will be holding back part of himself from you 'just in case'. The horse is not at your disposal, even if outwardly he appears to be doing exactly what you ask.

Establishing your personal space and beginning to direct your horse's movement consistently (see pages 100–102) will have removed some of his mental and emotional 'braces' as he becomes more sure of where he stands in your relationship. As a result, he will also have let go of some of his physical bracing. In short, your horse will have begun to relax.

Working directly on physical bracing will continue to release more mental braces, and your relationship with your horse will improve accordingly.

Ways to work on softness

Avoid making any of the mistakes listed in the box on page 109. This may take time, a change of mind-set and a lot of practice, but the effort will not be wasted and your horse's demeanour, behaviour and performance will improve. A good instructor will be able to provide you with help and support on the way.

It's simple

Never release on a brace – always release on softness.

There are many groundwork exercises you can use to start showing your horse that you are looking for softness from him, not bracing.

Backing up

Backing up is a good place to start working on softness with your horse. If he has already learned about your personal space and how to give to pressure applied to the lead rope, as you step towards him and take a feel on the rope (so that he experiences light pressure on his nose from the headcollar), he will most likely take a step back. Do this a couple more times, releasing the pressure on the rope each time he complies, and he will have understood the message: when you feel this touch on your nose, move your feet backwards.

However, you can also ask your horse to be soft at the same time as he moves his feet. As you apply pressure to the rope and your horse steps back, keep the pressure on and wait for him to

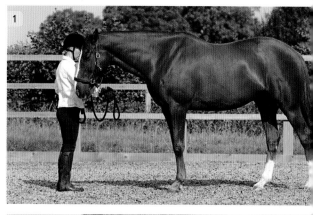

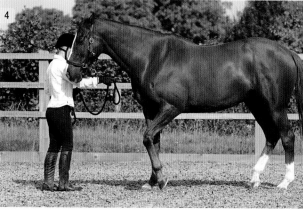

soften the muscles of his neck and drop his nose before releasing. When he does, you will be able to feel it through the rope as he 'lets go'.

It may take quite a number of backwards steps before your horse releases the brace in his neck and you can reward him. Do not give up: if you release before he softens, you will have taught him to brace.

Then look at the rest of your horse's body and the way he is stepping back. This time when you ask him to back up and soften, maintain pressure on the rope until the softness works through into the rest of his body. As he releases the muscles of his topline, his back will lift, he will start to use his abdominal muscles and his hindquarters to carry himself backwards instead of pushing stiffly with his front legs, and the movement will feel soft and almost effortless.

This is exactly what you want when you are riding. Moving in this way feels good to the horse too, so once he realizes he can, he will be happy to do so. As you work on this together, your horse will become increasingly settled mentally as well.

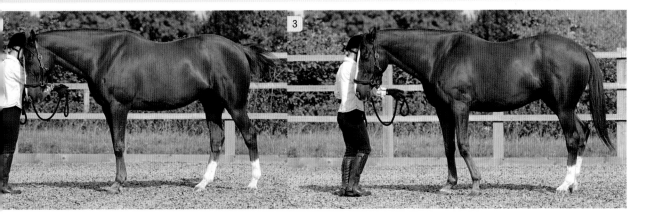

Other exercises

There are many other exercises you can do with your horse on the ground to help him become softer in his responses. A number of these are shown below and on page 112.

You do not need to do these exercises every day or for hours at a time, but if and when you choose to do one of them, make sure you work through to softness every time and do not reward your horse for bracing.

1) The handler is applying light pressure to the noseband of the headcollar via the lead rope, to ask the horse to step back. His response is to brace his neck and lean into the pressure. With all this weight on his forehand, he cannot begin to lift a forefoot and step back.

2) The handler keeps the same pressure on the headcollar, and the horse tries a different response: he drops his nose, softens his neck a little and begins to shift his weight back. This good try can be rewarded with a release.

3) The horse makes his first offer to step back – he is starting to make the connection between pressure on his nose and moving his feet. Again, he can be rewarded with a release.

4) His first steps are quite stiff and he has braced his neck and poked his nose once more…

5) …but then he begins to put everything together and steps back while also lightening his forehand a little and giving softly to the pressure. This is the time to release, pet the horse, and go and do something else for a while. As the horse becomes more proficient at this exercise, he will begin to lift his back and make more use of his abdominal muscles and hindquarters to carry himself easily backwards.

◁ It is a big deal for a horse to willingly soften and lower his head and neck to the ground to a cue from your hands, as he can feel extremely vulnerable in this position. When he manages this and finds he has survived, and that relaxing his neck has actually made him feel more comfortable rather than less, it can be used as a way to help settle him when he is anxious. You do not have to ask him to lower his head very far to achieve this effect, as long as he lets go of the tension in his neck. You can choose whatever cue you want to use: here, the handler has one hand on the noseband of the halter and the other resting lightly on the horse's poll. When teaching this exercise, remember to reward the slightest try in the right direction. The cue can be refined to just a touch on the top of the horse's neck, so that the handler does not have to bend down at all.

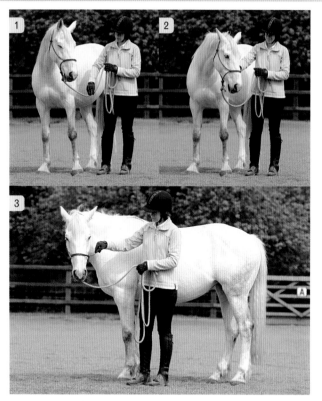

Less is more

It is surprisingly easy to slip into drilling your horse on exercises he has already mastered. We humans tend to want to repeat what is going well: 'That felt really good. Let's do it one more time. And one more.' For the horse, however, this can seem like punishment. He may start to offer different responses, convinced that he must have got it wrong, or continue to perform but switch off mentally. This is the exact opposite of what you want.

When your horse has done something really well, stop doing it. This way, he will know he has got it right and will be happy to repeat it on another day.

1) The handler puts a light feel on the rope to ask the horse to bring her head softly around to the side.

2) As the mare releases the muscles in her neck and poll in order to comply, this has a relaxing effect and her head also drops. Her movement alone has put slack in the rope so she has already rewarded herself, but the handler gives her a nice rub as well.

3) This side view shows that the horse's head is vertical: if she had tipped her nose up towards the handler she would have been using a different joint in her neck to do this and the action would not have produced the same relaxing effect.

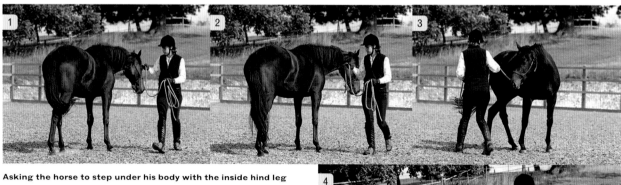

Asking the horse to step under his body with the inside hind leg has a relaxing effect on the muscles of the hind end, as well as on his state of mind as he responds softly to the request.

1) This mare looks settled and relaxed to begin with, so her response is likely to be relatively soft. The handler steps towards the mare's inside hind leg with intent...

2) ...and then brings her head around a little with just a suggestion from the rope, to give the her the idea that she should step her back end away.

3) The mare is already beginning to organize her hind legs in order to step over. From this angle, it is obvious that she has stepped well under her body with her inside hind leg. Next she will have to lift her inside foreleg and realign as her body straightens.

4) The mare responds to a suggestion with the rope by bending softly away and preparing to step her front end over.

LUNGEING

Lungeing is widely used for starting a youngster, to build in the cues he will need when ridden; for exercise and perhaps taking the steam out of a horse before riding; for building fitness and muscle; and for developing ways of moving, often with the use of training aids.

Lungeing can also be used to gain your horse's attention and increase communication between you, build your relationship, and help him to respond and move softly (see pages 91–94 and 109–112). In this way, lungeing can enhance your horse's understanding of what is required of him and engage his mind as well as his body.

Working on lungeing can also help you to read your horse and anticipate his actions (see page 99) and to learn more about using body language and positioning, energy and intent to influence his responses.

Working together

There are two ways of looking at lungeing (and, indeed, almost anything you do with your horse): you say and the horse does, or you say and then you both do it together. The first option gets the job done, but may not build much of a connection between you and your horse, sometimes even incorporating an adversarial element. The second option is much closer to what most of us would hope for under saddle, so it makes sense to do exactly the same on the ground.

Positioning

When you are working with your horse on the ground, obviously he can see you so where you position yourself in relation to him will have a big effect. If you ask your horse to move forward on the lunge line, you need to make sure you aren't inadvertently discouraging him from doing so by 'blocking' him with your body and then using heavier cues to try to get him moving. In this situation, some horses will eventually work out what you want, but others will find it extremely confusing and become increasingly anxious about the whole procedure.

Positioning yourself no further forward than your horse's inside hip will ensure that there is a big open space ahead of him into which he will naturally choose to move when you ask. Some horses will still move forward if you are positioned a little further towards their head, others may feel 'blocked' when you are barely in line with their girth area.

Make lungeing easy for yourself and your horse by checking that you are not creeping further forward relative to him as you go. Your horse – especially if he is a sensitive type – will tell you if you have, by slowing down or even stopping and trying to turn back the other way. This gives you a clue as to how to ask for those responses:
• Moving slightly further forward relative to your horse will signal to him to slow down.
• Moving further ahead again will ask him to stop.
• Moving forward until you are level with a point somewhere in front of his head will ask him to turn.

Movement and energy

As well as your positioning, you can use your own energy and movement to convey to the horse what you want him to do. This type of communication can become extremely subtle, so that onlookers can barely see what you are doing. Your horse, too, will appreciate your use of almost imperceptible cues, which will allow him to respond more calmly, smoothly and softly to your requests. You are beginning to synchronize your movement and energy with those of your horse, and his with yours (see pages 45 and 104–105).

Practising controlling your own energy in this way will also have benefits when you are in the saddle, as it gives you yet another way to communicate with your horse: he may not be able to *see* you, but he will be able to *feel* you increase and decrease the energy in your body and will respond accordingly.

At its simplest, on the lunge line if you want your horse to:
• **Stand still** Stand still yourself and relax. This can be quite difficult for some of us to do for more than a few seconds, so it is hardly surprising that the horse is 'busy' too. Practise both of you standing still for gradually increasing amounts of time (see also page 140).
• **Move forward in walk** Raise your own energy a little, give the cue and then walk forward yourself with your horse. For a faster walk, increase the energy of your own walk; for a slower walk, do the opposite. Most horses will respond to your energy and movement alone, but if yours does not, you can add in a cue (such as a click of your tongue for faster, or light pressure on the line for slower). After a few repetitions, he will begin to respond to your energy alone. Practise changing the speed within the walk so that you are setting the pace, not your horse.
• **Move forward in trot** Raise you energy further and walk more briskly. Again, practise changing the speed within the trot.
• **Downward transitions** To move from trot to walk, lower your energy and walk more slowly. To halt from either walk or trot, lower your energy to give your horse a brief warning that a change is coming, then stop moving.

As well as thinking about your energy and speed of movement, remember to check that your positioning is appropriate for what you are asking your horse to do.

All these things, and more, are fun to practise and refine, and will get you and your horse communicating and working more closely together.

Communication on the lunge

This horse is inexperienced at lungeing. He has also not yet come to terms with his handlers making decisions about speed and direction rather than himself. This sequence demonstrates many of the reactions that are typical of a horse in this situation. With careful practice, he will learn to pay more consistent attention to the handler and respond more promptly and willingly to her cues, which can then become more subtle. He will also learn that he should respond to a feel on the lunge line by softening instead of bracing, and that he should work to bend around the handler in order to keep slack in the line at all times.

1) Lungeing from an ordinary headcollar, the horse is walking forward quietly but pulling on the line as the handler asks him to bend into the circle. The position of his left ear indicates that part of his attention is on the open space to that side and he would probably like to move into it.

2) The handler raises her energy, opens out her posture and then flicks the free loop of the lunge line to ask the horse to move into a trot.

5) The handler lowers her energy and slows her pace to ask the horse to walk, and he looks as if he is about to respond relatively softly...

6) ...but instead he carries on trotting and braces into the tightening lunge line.

3) Once the horse is trotting, the handler continues to walk purposefully but is able to soften her posture and still maintain the pace. The horse is beginning to work with more concentration and his body posture is softer, but he needs to soften further in order to bend more around the circle.

4) As the horse comes around to the open part of the arena, the handler again opens her posture to keep his attention and prevent him drifting out to his left.

7) This brings the horse to a walk, but because he braced against the lunge line before making the transition he continues to do so in walk.

8) Similarly, as the handler stops her feet to ask the horse to halt, he pushes on into the lunge line.

Transitions and turns

When lungeing, it is a good plan to make lots of transitions:

• Move from one pace to another.
• Change the speed within the same pace.
• Move from halt to walk, trot or canter, and back to halt.

This will keep your horse's attention on you as he waits for your next instruction, and cause him to think about what he is doing and how he is moving as he prepares to make shifts of balance at each transition. In this way, you and your horse will be communicating throughout: it is all too easy for a horse to trot round and round on the lunge without engaging mentally with the proceedings at all.

Turns are also 'transitions': your horse is moving one way, then he has to respond to your cue and organize himself to turn and move in the opposite direction. This is only possible with set-ups of the lunge line that allow for the horse to be moving in either direction, and the horse will need to turn inwards to avoid getting wrapped up in the line. If your horse has learned about your personal space, and you take care to get your positioning correct, you need not worry that asking him to turn inwards will encourage him to come right up to you.

Short-line lungeing

Lungeing on a shorter line – usually about 3.75m (12ft) – can make it easier to teach your horse about turns, among other things. He will be closer to you, so:

• It will be easier to get his attention.
• Maintaining your personal space becomes more important, so you will need to learn how to use the line and your body position accurately to signal to your horse where he should be. A good instructor will be able to help you with this.
• As the horse turns, he will need to move his hindquarters and then his forehand (see page 110), and curve softly around your personal space as he does so.

Remember pressure and release

Pressure from behind

It is not that uncommon to see a horse being 'chased' around on the lunge. In other words, instead of giving a cue and then releasing when the horse does as asked – he moves into trot, say – the handler continues to give the same cue intermittently even when the horse is already trotting. The result is either a confused horse, one that becomes dull and unenthusiastic or unresponsive to the cue, or one that does as required but mentally leaves the situation.

Pressure from in front

The other way in which pressure is often applied inadvertently during lungeing is through the lunge line. When the horse does as asked – again, take the example of moving forward into trot – it's important that he isn't discouraged from complying by then running into a tight lunge line.

The line should remain slack whenever the horse is doing what he has been asked to. He will then be able to feel it when pressure is applied to the line and search for the answer that will release that pressure. For example, the horse:

• Turns his head and neck to the outside of the circle, taking his attention away from his handler.
• Starts to pull outwards on the circle away from his handler.
• Rushes forward at a faster speed than requested by his handler.

In each instance, if the line was previously slack the horse will feel it tighten as he puts pressure on it himself and will begin to look for a release by changing what he is doing. If the line is tight all the time, he won't bother.

A tight lunge line also restricts the way the horse is able to move and balance himself on the circle. It will cause him to brace his muscles and move crookedly, and over time he may suffer physical problems as a result.

• On the smaller circle, the horse will gradually learn that the easiest way to move is softly and with adequate bend in his body.

As long as the lunge line remains slack whenever the horse is doing as asked, the fact that he is on a smaller circle should not place him under undue physical strain. It is the tight lunge line, on any size of circle, that causes the horse to move unnaturally and puts his body at risk. However, as with all lungeing, some common sense guidelines apply:

• Keep sessions short.

• Stay in walk to begin with, incorporating turns and walk–halt–walk transitions, until your horse understands what is required and is moving softly and with adequate bend.

• Even when he is able to work in faster paces as well, the majority of the work should still be in walk.

1) This experienced and compliant mare presents a very different picture to the horse on pages 114–115. She circles softly in walk...

2) ...and in trot on a short lunge line. Note the slack in the line as she bends around the handler.

3) The mare's inside hind leg steps well under as the handler asks her to start the turn.

4) She then brings her front end across...

5) ...and steps off onto the right rein, bending away from the handler to move around her personal space.

6) She trots off quietly around the circle, again maintaining the slack in the line. Her willing concentration – 'inner softness' if you like – is apparent throughout and she has placed her whole self at the handler's disposal.

1) The handler makes sure this mare is moving with sufficient impulsion to take the log jump that is up ahead.

2) The horse sights the jump and the handler leaves her to it – she does not pull on the lunge line or try to adjust the horse's stride in any way.

3) The horse takes the jump herself in good style. Once your horse is experienced at lunging in an arena, taking opportunities like this to add variety and new challenges to the work will increase your horse's confidence and help to build a really solid understanding between you.

LONG-LINING

Long-lining is often used when preparing a youngster for riding, as a follow-on to lungeing. Using a bit and two lines, you can teach him the rudiments of stop, go, turn and back in a way that simulates what will happen when he is ridden, and get him out and about before beginning to hack him out.

As with lungeing (see page 113), long-lining can also be used to gain your horse's attention, improve the communication between you and build your relationship further, whatever his age and experience. It is another opportunity for you to practise reading your horse, getting your timing accurate, increasing and decreasing your own energy and more. In addition, long-lining is a good way to start using your own focus to direct your horse.

Before you begin

Most horses will react to some degree the first time they feel a line behind their hindquarters, so before you attach two lines to your horse and begin working at long-lining it is a wise precaution to get him used to this feel!

1) Standing on the near side, the handler places the lunge line around the mare's off side and hindquarters, staying well out of the kick zone. She then asks the horse to move her forehand to the right and her hindquarters to the left, by applying a light feel to the line. By looking at the horse's left eye and angling her body towards the horse's forehand, the handler helps her to understand that she should move her front end away.

2) The horse begins the manoeuvre, and the handler makes sure that she is still well out of the kick zone.

3) At this point the mare is moving her hindquarters away from the handler and her forehand towards her. Note the slack in the line – this exercise does not involve pulling the horse around the turn – and the soft bend through the horse's body. The manoeuvre will be complete when the mare is facing the handler. She should stop there, without pushing forward into the handler's space. The mare clearly has no problem with the feel of the line around her hindquarters, but remember to check this out on both sides.

Positioning, movement and energy

The use of positioning, movement and energy are the same for long-lining as for lungeing (see pages 113–114).

Many people use long-lining primarily to get a young horse out on lanes and tracks without being led, and consequently position themselves directly behind him. However, it is easier for your horse to begin learning this new skill on a circle, with which he is already familiar from lungeing, with you using the same positioning and cues as before. Co-ordinate these with the use of light pressure on the lines and your horse should find it relatively easy to learn to respond to cues through the bit to slow down, halt, back up and turn – the turn is outwards this time to avoid him getting tangled in the lines.

The blind spot and changing eyes

As your horse makes his first turns on the long lines, you may notice that as he reaches the point in the turn where you disappear in the blind spot behind him he becomes a little concerned. This is similar to what happens when you get on a young horse for the first time and parts of you disappear and suddenly reappear in his other eye, so it is a good idea for him to get used to this while you are on the ground!

It is also one reason why some horses – even experienced riding horses – become anxious if you start teaching long-lining from a position directly behind them: at least to begin with, it makes it easier on the horse if he can see you and respond to your positioning, movement and energy just as he did on the lunge.

1) This horse is being long-lined off an ordinary headcollar, with the lines threaded through the stirrups (which are joined together below his belly using a stirrup leather). Although they are moving on a straight line, the handler is on a track slightly to the left of the horse, so that he can still see her.

2) The handler asks the horse to turn to the right by 'pushing' on the horse's left eye with her body position and putting light pressure on the right-hand line.

3) She switches sides and the horse moves off calmly to the right – he clearly had no problem with her 'disappearing' as she crossed through the blind spot behind him.

1) When long-lining out and about, to start with it helps to have an assistant to guide the horse when required, until he understands what is expected. Even when he is going well 'solo', for safety's sake it is a good idea to have a second person along who can go to the horse's head if necessary.

2) The assistant has dropped back and the horse quickly becomes distracted and a little tense without a leader to follow. However, if the handler remains calm and in a position where the horse can see her, he will soon settle back to the task in hand.

Working together using focus

Once your horse is working happily on a circle, you can move on to long-lining him around the arena in any pattern you like, practising increases and decreases in speed, turns, halts, transitions and so on as you go. (As you both become more proficient, you can also try manoeuvres such as leg yielding, backing up on a curve, or anything else you fancy.)

Working around the bigger space, your horse is more likely to lose concentration, but a little tweak on the inside line when this happens should be enough to bring him back to you. Alternatively, asking him to make a transition or turn will get his mind back on the job.

More subtly, you can also start to use your own focus to engage your horse's, so that eventually you both focus on the same place and move there together – this is what you want when riding (see page 151).

It's *your* job to steer

When you start long-lining your horse around the arena, and especially to targets (see box opposite), you may be surprised to discover that he has very little 'built-in' steering. If you stop concentrating, he will wander off course, as at this stage he has no idea that you require him to move in a straight line.

We tend to assume that somehow the horse 'knows' instinctively that he should move directly from A to B, or all the way around the outside track, and is being deliberately awkward when he veers away. On the contrary: it is your responsibility to show him what is required.

1) This mare is being long-lined around the arena off a bridle and without a surcingle or saddle. One of the advantages of this method is that the lines run directly to the handler's hands and one or other can be taken out to the side if necessary to indicate direction more clearly to a less experienced horse.

2) One of the disadvantages is that the horse can swing out underneath the outside line, which then lies over the mare's neck rather than around her hindquarters.

3) There is little the handler can do now except stay calm and...

4) ...step ahead of the horse (but not directly in front of her) to turn her onto the other rein, thereby restoring the lines to their correct position and carrying on immediately with the work.

Waiting for softness

As you work with your horse on the long lines, it is important that every time you signal to him through the bit – to turn, stop, back up and so on – you wait for him to give softly to it before offering a release. If you release simply for him turning, stopping or stepping backwards, you will be encouraging him to brace his muscles as he does so. Remember: never release on a brace – always release on softness (see page 110).

1) This horse is learning to back up on long lines. He is stepping back but also bracing his neck and poking his nose against the pressure of the lines.

2) The horse has put slack in the lines by softening a little with his head and neck. The handler can build on this to achieve a soft, flowing back-up.

Using targets

A good way to begin engaging your horse's focus by using your own is to long-line him to targets. These can be anything you like: cones dotted about the arena, dressage markers, coloured lead ropes tied to the fence and so on.

Focus on your first target and guide your horse towards it. When he arrives there, ask him to stop and then use the lines to encourage him to touch it with his nose. Horses find this surprisingly easy if you provide accurate signals. Then focus on your next target, guide your horse to it and ask him to touch it. It will not take long before your horse starts to look for the next target himself, and he will take his cue as to which this is from your focus, backed up by your steering on the long lines. Once you have pointed him in the right direction, at some point you will feel him 'lock on' to the target and take you both to it.

At this stage, you can start to move your horse on to the next target just as he reaches the first one, before he gets as far as touching it. Before long, you will be moving him easily wherever you like, simply by focusing on the next point you want to move towards and indicating the direction through the lines.

This, and other similar ways of working, have an important effect on your horse: they give what you are doing a purpose that he can understand and with which he can become involved. This greatly improves his motivation and concentration. It also teaches you to concentrate, think, look ahead and focus on where you are going rather than on the horse (see page 133). To begin with you may be shocked at just how tiring all this is, but it is worth the effort to persevere, as these are all skills you will need when riding.

1) The mare is being long-lined to cones around the arena and has already 'locked on' to her target.

2) As she gets closer to the cone, she naturally veers to one side to try to avoid knocking into it...

3) ...and then, as the handler tries to steer her she moves back, to the other side.

4) With some careful and patient steering from the handler, the horse eventually realizes she should line up with the cone, and her natural curiosity then leads her to touch it with her nose.

5) A little later in the session the mare locks on and takes the handler to the target quite happily...

6) ...but this time as they reach the cone the handler steers the horse past...

7) ...and around it, then immediately on to find the next target.

LOOSE WORK

Loose work is often used to give horses a chance to let off steam before a training session begins and to teach them to jump without the encumbrance of a rider. Just like lungeing and long-lining (see pages 113 and 118), loose work can also be used to gain your horse's attention, increase communication and build your relationship.

Safety first

If a horse has learned to become aggressive in response to people, is inclined to run you over or in any other way seems likely to threaten your physical safety, you will need to seek professional help. Do not attempt to work him loose on your own.

1) The horse is virtually ignoring the handler as he walks around the pen, and almost all his attention is on what is going on outside – although he *is* walking, so must be aware of her presence!

2) The handler raises her energy and flicks the lunge line to get the horse to focus on her, and he immediately starts to pay her more attention.

5) ...into a fast canter...

6) ...flinging his head up and down. His reaction suggests that the handler has used a little too much pressure (in the horse's opinion!) to send him forward.

What loose work can teach your horse

It can make a big impression on a horse if you are able to direct him without a physical connection. This is especially true of those that have learned to ignore your actions or direct *you* instead!

For a horse that has been lunged and/or long-lined in a way which has taught him that his job is simply to trot round and round on 'automatic pilot', loose work may be a good way to start opening up the lines of communication. The mere fact that it is something different to what he is used to doing can make it easier to change established patterns of behaviour. Once he is beginning to work *with* you, instead of on his own, lungeing or long-lining can be reintroduced if you like, and it should then be easier to change his way of going in those situations, too.

Round or square?

A safe enclosure is the first prerequisite for loose work. This can be round or square/rectangular and each has its advantages:

Round pen
• Easier to prevent the horse getting 'stuck' as there are no corners.
• Portable models are widely available.

Square/rectangular pen
• Horse has to rebalance himself slightly as he takes each corner, so helping him to develop physically.
• Tends to have a less 'dizzying' effect on the handler (and possibly the horse).

3) The handler steps forward with intent and the horse moves into trot. But he is quite tense, and…

4) …a couple of strides later he explodes forward…

7) …Next time around the handler has taken note of the horse's feedback and reduced her cues, and the horse proceeds in a strong but slightly more relaxed trot without leaping forward.

Take care

Unfortunately, loose work can sometimes degenerate into the handler chasing the horse around to little purpose. In addition, if movement is repeatedly used as a correction or punishment, so that when the horse makes a 'mistake' he is sent away from the handler to move fast around the pen or enclosure, this can have the effect of teaching the horse to shut down mentally, to run from his handler and that his job is to keep moving at all costs. A good instructor will be able to help you avoid these pitfalls and develop subtle communication with your horse.

What loose work teaches you

Because you no longer have a physical connection with or control over your horse, loose work will push you to develop all the skills you have already learned during lungeing and long-lining. It will help you to:

• Direct your horse's movement even more precisely.
• Find other ways to gain his attention now that you cannot use pressure on the lunge or long lines.
• Use the full range of your own movement and energy as necessary to change his speed, pace or direction.
• Improve your timing and positioning – now, one wrong move and he's gone!
• Adjust your body language, energy and focus to bring your horse to you and cause him to want to stay with you.
• Be able to move him away from you equally easily, without him becoming tense and/or fleeing.

By working on these, you will continue to refine the ways in which your movement, intent, energy and focus become synchronized with those of your horse, and vice versa (see page 45). All this is good practice in making use of these lines of communication when you are riding.

Checking your relationship

Working your horse loose will also show you where the relationship between you is really at, as he can leave not just mentally but also physically (at least within the confines of the enclosure) if he wants to! You can therefore use loose work from time to time to check on your horse's training, aiming for him – and you – to become more attentive, smoother, calmer and softer in everything you do together.

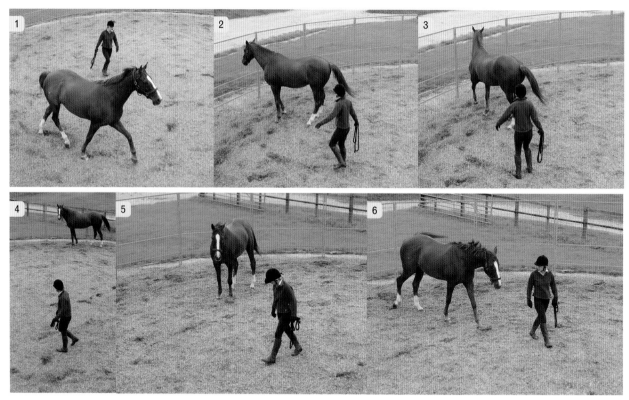

1) The handler is in position to send the horse forward into the open space in front of him.

2) To turn him back the other way, she steps ahead of him (but not directly in front) and focuses on his left eye to 'push' him away…

3) …into the now open space to the right.

4) The handler has turned the horse once more. She drops her energy and steps away from the horse to invite him to step towards her. The horse looks at the handler, considering the situation, but does not move.

5) The handler begins to walk away and the horse turns and moves tentatively towards her. Another way to invite the horse to do this would be to remain facing him and, keeping your energy low, step back away from him.

6) Now he has made his decision and follows the handler.

MAKE YOUR HORSE BRAVE

For safety's sake, we do not want horses to be spooking, shying, fleeing or in any other way 'losing the plot' when they are with people. This is common sense: horses are large, powerful, fast-moving animals that can cause major accidents when they act on raw instinct alone.

1) The horse is curious about the strange object to his left, but is also a little fearful and ready to move away into the open space on his right, as fear wins over curiosity.

2) The handler keeps the plastic close to the horse, so that he learns that moving away does not get rid of the 'monster'. She maintains a relaxed, quiet demeanour in order not to become part of the horse's problem herself by appearing to chase him. Nor does she restrict him with the lead rope, unless he tries to leave the situation entirely.

3) The instant that the horse offers to stop moving away, the handler removes the plastic from his proximity. Although he is still wary and tense, he is beginning to realize that moving his feet is not the answer to his dilemma.

4) The horse is becoming more relaxed, and the handler is able to move the plastic towards and away from him without him trying to flee. She gives him a rub as an extra reward for this big try.

5) The horse is now at the stage where he will tolerate the plastic being rubbed against his skin. Ideally, the handler will work with him for a little longer, until he lowers his head and really relaxes, showing that he has fully understood and accepted the day's lesson.

Introducing scary objects to your horse

You can make your horse less reactive to sudden or unusual noises, unfamiliar feelings on his skin and the sudden appearance of scary objects close to him by using 'approach and retreat' (see page 67).

A plastic bag, perhaps attached to a stick, is a good first tool to use for this: it makes a crackling noise, feels strange on the horse's skin and flaps around in a scary way. The object is not to frighten your horse witless, nor to 'desensitize' him.

• You want him to learn to accept the object calmly on all parts of his body and when it is waved around close to him. Eventually, you also want him to cope when the object appears suddenly from any direction.

• You do not want him to feel trapped into standing motionless while he is still afraid, as in this situation he may 'shut down' mentally – and a horse that does this can suddenly 'wake up' to what is going on and react accordingly!   (cont.)

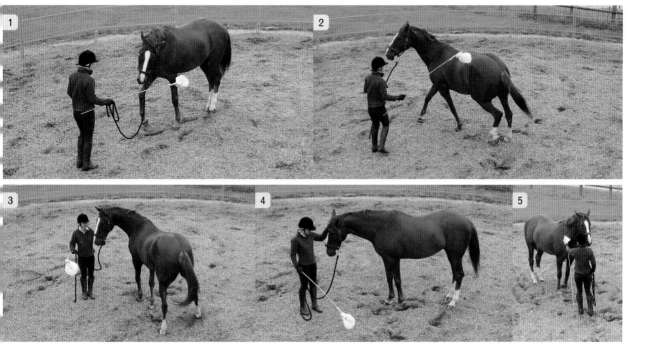

- **You want him** to learn the difference between you simply stroking his body or passing the object around him in a relaxed manner (when you would like him to stand still) and using it with energy and intent (when you would like him to move off).
- **You do not want** to desensitize your horse so successfully that he never reacts to anything ever again, including your cues!

Once your horse has accepted the plastic bag, it should be relatively easy to work in the same way with several other objects, such as a flappy towel, brightly coloured umbrella or noisy sports rattle. After all this, your horse should be ready to take most unfamiliar sights, sounds and feels in his stride!

A safe relationship

The first point to remember is that when a horse reacts instinctively he is not being 'stupid' or acting dangerously on purpose to frighten or annoy you. He is behaving as nature intended and trying to put distance between himself and anything scary (including that tiny scrap of plastic or odd-coloured fallen leaf) that in his mind might just try to eat him.

One reason for building a solid relationship with your horse is so that he doesn't see you as something scary, to which he needs to react in an instinctive way when the going gets tough. You will both be better off if your horse sees you as a place of safety and looks for direction from you, rather than taking his own decisions when he is anxious (see page 98).

Learning about your personal space and how to lead properly will help to prevent your horse leaping on top of you when he is startled, so make sure these are well in place before you start helping him to face his fears (see pages 100 and 103–06).

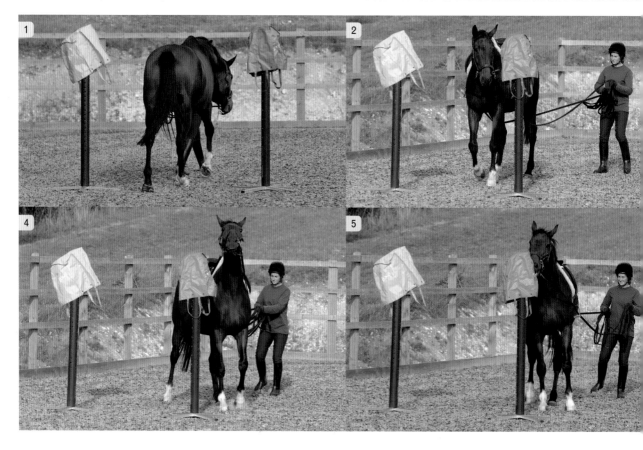

Introducing your horse to scary objects

There will be times when you are out riding that you will need your horse to move past, through, over or under something that he finds frightening. This might include a dog barking unseen behind a garden wall, a rushing stream, a narrow bridge or a fallen tree.

If you can introduce your horse to hazards that cause him a similar level of anxiety and can help him to deal calmly with the situation in the arena – where you have control of all the variables – you will be in a much better position to tackle such hazards when you are out and about.

You may not be able to divert a stream through the arena for training purposes, but you can use a variety of everyday items to create a comparable situation. For example:
• Asking your horse to walk over an old carpet, plastic tarpaulin, sheet of plywood and so on is good preparation for any 'false ground' you may meet when hacking. This includes deep puddles, streams, a wooden bridge, heavy mud – in fact, any ground conditions that may cause your horse to worry about losing his footing or becoming trapped.

1) With the gap between the scary posts relatively wide, the horse leads through easily.

2) On long lines, the horse is tackling the obstacle more 'on his own'. He takes a good look at the green bag, but appears to be on his way through the gap anyway…

3) …then suddenly stops and investigates the yellow bag. He is still concentrating on the problem and trying to work out how to deal with it, and as he does so the handler moves both herself and the lines to try to get his attention back on the gap through which she wants him to walk.

4) The horse decides this is too much to ask and tries to duck out to the left, to go around the obstacle…

5) …but the handler stops him – and he quickly takes the opportunity to re-examine the green bag.

6) This time, as soon as the handler gets the horse's attention on the gap between the posts he decides he can make it and walks through quite calmly.

7) With all this preparation, once the rider is on board the horse walks quietly through at the first time of asking.

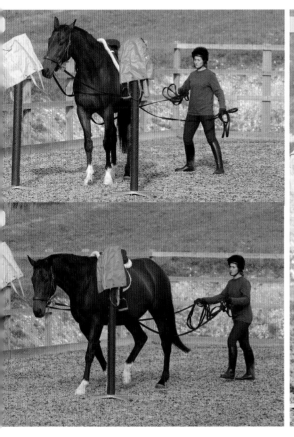

• Setting up barrels, jump stands, cones with flags on top and so on (all of which can be scary in themselves) and asking your horse to walk through an increasingly narrow space between them will help him learn to deal with narrow gateways and other situations where space is tight.

• Traffic is an unavoidable hazard, so if you are at all unsure of your horse's reaction check this out in the arena first. Build up slowly from, say, a stationary car with the engine turned off and plenty of space for him to get past, gradually increasing the noise and speed of the car and the tightness of the passing space. If you have access to a large vehicle such as a van or tractor, so much the better! Get your horse used to vehicles approaching him from both front and rear; following a vehicle that is driving away from him can make a big difference to his confidence, as he will feel he is chasing it rather than the other way round.

Remember...

When you are working with your horse to help him feel braver, bear in mind the principles you have learned so far, including:

• The importance of your *attitude*: stay calm and positive, and think of helping your horse learn rather than making him do it (see box on page 88, and page 98).

• *Approach and retreat*: this is how horses teach themselves about scary objects, so make appropriate use of it (see page 67).

• Keeping your horse's *attention* on you and where you are both heading, not the approaching hazard (see pages 91–93).

• Correct use of *pressure and release*: this is how you help, support and direct your horse through tricky situations (see pages 95–98).

Making progress

Once your horse is doing well when you are leading him, you can progress to lungeing and/or long-lining him through or over hazards. In this way, he learns to tackle the obstacle 'on his own', while still accepting your direction – this time from behind. Finally, you can ride him through, past and over the same hazards.

1) This Icelandic horse has had lots of training with unusual obstacles, and her rider can take her virtually anywhere safe in the knowledge that she will cope. She walks straight onto the plastic – although she feels the need to investigate it more closely and the rider allows her to do so by giving her the rein.

It's all about building your relationship

As your relationship with your horse becomes more solid, you will not have to continue to introduce new 'hazards' forever. He will increasingly trust that if you say something is fine, it will be, and he can safely and calmly do what you ask.

This means that you do not have to rush to work your horse through situations he finds really confronting: this is not 'giving in' or 'letting the horse win'. Wait for a while, until you have built up your relationship in other ways and tackled some less scary obstacles successfully, and you may find he no longer has a problem with the bigger ones.

Equally, asking your horse to cope with what he finds difficult or scary but not impossibly so, and supporting him all the way through, can in itself help to enhance the relationship between the two of you.

2) On the next pass, from the opposite direction, she is even less concerned…

3) …and she is more than happy to trot over calmly at the first time of asking.

1) First time between the scary posts, which are set quite close together, and the mare glances briefly at the yellow bag.

2) Next time around, with the posts even closer together, she is completely unfazed.

3) At the mare's first encounter with the windmills, she is so unconcerned that she actually touches the spinning sails with her nose to check them out.

4) She is equally happy to walk past them, just far enough away to accommodate the rider's leg.

4 UNDERSTANDING YOUR HORSE FROM THE SADDLE

This chapter is not intended as an A–Z of how to ride and train your horse. Instead, it looks at ways to communicate with your horse from the saddle that make sense to him and allow him to comply easily with your requests. By applying an understanding of the horse's viewpoint to varied examples of common riding situations, the aim is that eventually you will be able to work out effective strategies for yourself.

WHO DOES WHAT?

When riding, generally it is our job to do most of the thinking and the horse's job to do most of the physical work. We decide where to go, how fast and in what manner, and we borrow the horse's power, speed, energy and athleticism to do it. And yet the situation often ends up the other way round: the horse makes the decisions and the rider works hard physically to change his mind! But it doesn't have to be like this.

The rider's role

As a rider, your main responsibility is to learn to ride as well as you can. First and foremost, this means learning how the horse moves and then practising sitting in balance and 'going with' that movement, so that you hinder your horse as little as possible in his job of carrying you. Sessions on a simulator machine under the guidance of a good instructor can be of great value here (and kinder to the horse!).

A game of two halves

When the horse moves, in each gait he sets his feet down in a particular sequence and his body swings along in a specific way 'independently', as the rider you need to do the same with your own body – luckily, the part that allows you to sit on the horse is also built in two halves!

Most people manage this fairly easily at a walk – after all, this is how we walk ourselves – but once the horse moves up through the gaits and the movement becomes bigger our natural reaction is to tighten up and move both sides of our body together, as one block. We are now going against the movement of the horse, making it difficult for him to move freely and softly. Learning to go with the horse's movement at all gaits is your top priority.

Once you can do this (which will feel to the horse as if you are doing nothing), when you then ask him to do something, he will actually notice!

> ### Towards collection
>
> For your horse to:
> - let go of any bracing in his body and move softly...
> - release tension in the muscles of his neck and back...
> - start using his abdominal muscles for support instead...
>   ...you will have to do the same.
>
> (For more about collection, see pages 165–167.)

From groundwork to riding

You can now take all the important principles you have learned about how to communicate with and teach a horse on the ground (see Chapter 3) into your ridden work. The situation should not change just because you have left terra firma, although it may become a little more challenging:

- Instead of being able to see what your horse is doing, you will have to rely more on feel.
- Your own energy level, focus and intent remain important in influencing your horse, but their use and effects can be more difficult to grasp in the beginning (see box opposite).
- The way in which you breathe will have a big effect on both you and your horse: tight, shallow breaths will cause tension and even fear; deep, slow breaths will produce confidence and relaxation.
- Your attitude will transmit even more directly to your horse, through unconscious changes in your body.

1) With the human and horse movement synchronized, we can see that they walk in essentially the same way: as the right leg steps forward, the right hip drops and the left hip rises.

2) As left leg steps forward, the left hip drops and the right hip rises. All this is important information for learning to synchronize your movement with that of your horse when you are in the saddle.

Energy, focus, intent

A rider is wandering slowly around the arena on her horse, which appears listless and uninterested in proceedings. The same rider makes small adjustments and the horse immediately starts to move with purpose and interest. This is the effect of a difference in energy, focus and intent:

• In the first example the rider sits slackly in the saddle, focusing on the horse's head, and has no belief in – or urgency about – getting the job done.

• The rider in the second example has plenty of energy within her body (even though she makes no big movements), looks up and ahead to where she is going, and has no doubt that she and the horse will get there.

△ Riding along the side of the arena in walk, there is little urgency for the rider to look where she is going and her gaze has become fixed on the horse's head. Without direction, the horse is slowing down – so the rider is working hard to keep him going and the horse is bracing against her heavy cues.

◁ Turning into the middle of the arena in canter, the rider must now concentrate on providing direction and focus, and moving forward at speed – and the horse is mirroring her exactly (just as he did when she stared at his head).

Priorities

Just as in groundwork, if you make your first priority to try always to keep your horse attentive, calm and soft, then all other goals – dressage movements, jumping, hacking out safely and enjoyably – will follow in the course of training. Conversely, without these basics in place everything will be a struggle to some degree, for both you and your horse.

When riding, you should be signalling to the horse what he is to do next and then *allowing him to do it*, not physically pushing and pulling him around. Remember: you provide the brains, he provides the brawn.

The horse's role

The horse already knows how to do everything we ask of him: even a day-old foal has mastered all the gaits, can turn at speed and changes leads at will. We just need to show him that we want him to do all this on cue – this is training.

The onus is therefore on you, the rider/trainer, *not* the horse, to create the communication and understanding between the two of you that will ultimately lead to the performance you want.

How miscommunications arise

The horse learns under saddle in exactly the same way as he does when you are on the ground (see pages 95–99). He also becomes confused, reluctant, anxious or fearful for exactly the same reasons – poor rider attitude, inconsistency, heavy cues, mis-timed releases, no release at all – and sitting on a horse in this state is not always a good place to be.

The better your riding skills become, the less likely you are to miscommunicate with your horse *inadvertently* by bouncing in the saddle, going against his movement, breathing poorly, and tensing or moving bits of your body without realizing.

When wrong becomes right

Remember that your horse will always seek to find a release from pressure of any kind, so if he is consistently offering a response you don't want, first check that he is not finding a release by doing so – and that you are giving him a release when he offers the behaviour you do want.

A common example is the horse that flings his head in the air, yanks it downwards or tucks his nose to his chest in response

△ **Within hours of birth, a foal can already perform all the gaits, transitions and movements we will eventually ask of him under saddle. This young colt revels in travelling at speed – it is this enthusiasm for using his body well that we want to preserve when we start developing him as a riding horse.**

to even light pressure on the bit. All these actions produce a release for the horse, by either putting slack in the reins or pulling them through the rider's hands, so he will repeat them. Their origin often lies in heavy-handed riding with no release when the horse tries to soften to the bit (see pages 144–147), until out of desperation he contrives to produce a release for himself. After a number of repetitions, with the same result, the horse will conclude that his response is the one the rider wants: he thinks he is doing what is right, while the rider thinks the exact opposite.

Clear, consistent communication is the key to successful riding and training, and the rest of this chapter aims to show how this may be achieved in a variety of situations, as well as how miscommunications arise in different ways.

1) This ex-racehorse tries to give himself a release from rein pressure by bracing his neck and pushing hard on the bit...

2) ...lifting his head high and bringing it back towards the rider...

3) ...or dropping his head and curling his nose in – if necessary right back to his chest. The horse has managed to put slack in the reins with the last two actions, so will continue to look for a release in these ways. However, this rider is well aware of the situation and knows that her task now is to reschool him to understand that the release is actually to be found somewhere else (see pages 144–147).

RIDING IN AN ARENA

Many riders profess to find working in an arena or other schooling area dull and boring, and believe their horse does, too. They prefer to get straight on with hacking, galloping and jumping – and then wonder why problems gradually begin to emerge in their horse's behaviour and way of going.

△ This arena shows several features that may cause a horse to behave differently in different areas. The aspect is open on three sides, but the bank of trees and shrubs on the left can act as a 'pressure', causing horses to lose concentration as they approach that side, veer away from the fence, or spook as they reach the corner. The gate is a natural draw for horses, but the jumps and other equipment are also stored here, which may counteract this effect.

Why use an arena?

Of course, you can school a horse while hacking, but it's human nature not to bother too much once you are out enjoying a ride! In addition, an arena has a number of advantages:

• It provides a safe, enclosed area, with plenty of space on good footing.

• There are generally fewer distractions, so it is easier to keep your horse's attention (and your own) on the job in hand.

• There are no outside influences (cars, pedestrians, dogs and so on) that are beyond your control, so you can work exactly as you and your horse need to at any given moment. This is extremely important if training is to be consistent – if you change the way you are riding because a car is approaching or there is a plastic bag caught in the hedge, your horse will quickly become confused (see page 95).

The arena is the ideal place to prepare your horse to face the outside world: it is unfair (and can rapidly become unsafe) to expect him to cope with everything he will encounter while out and about unless he has undergone good basic training in a less challenging environment. If you don't have access to an arena, try to find a safe, relatively flat field with good footing to school in.

From the horse's point of view

To the horse, the arena is an alien environment. Unless he is very experienced, do not assume he somehow 'knows' how he should work within it: it is your job to show him what you require.

For example, working around the outside track at the same distance from the fence and at the same gait and speed all the way round may seem an absurd idea to your horse:

• At first, most horses will naturally move more freely towards the gate than away from it, not because they are lazy and want to avoid work (see box below, and page 139) but because they feel unsure in an unfamiliar environment and are drawn towards the exit, which leads back to familiarity and their herd mates.

• There may be a 'spooky' corner – one where there are dark shadows, or perhaps where the scary jump stands are stored – and the horse will probably wish to give this a wide berth.

• The perimeter fence (and especially walls in a covered arena) may be experienced by the horse as a 'pressure' pushing him towards the centre, where there is ample open space and he can be sure nothing is going to jump out at him. Insisting that your horse work on the outside track from the outset is usually counterproductive. Try *helping* him:

• If your horse does is comfortable at the far end of the arena, work nearer the gate and gradually increase your distance from it until he remains calm in all areas.

• If he veers off the track at a particular spot, circle him off it yourself before he reaches that point and gradually take him closer to it during the course of your session, until he can remain calm as he travels past it.

Neither of these approaches is 'giving in to the horse'. While you might be able to *make* him travel around the outside track, this addresses the symptoms, not the cause. You will therefore have to *make* him keep to the track every time you ride. In addition, you cannot actually accomplish any meaningful work with a horse that is tense and anxious.

Instead, if you work primarily on keeping your horse attentive, calm and soft (see page 138), as his confidence grows he will begin to *offer* to work quietly in any area of the arena you choose. This approach applies equally to a horse that is inclined to cling to the perimeter fence.

Stay consistent

Do not change the way you ride just because you are in an arena – this is extremely unfair on your horse. Many riders stiffen and try to make things happen, 'create' impulsion, drive the horse forward, push and pull him into a correct bend and so on, but these tactics generally have the opposite effect on the horse! If a horse knows that whenever he enters the arena he will be subjected to heavy cues and probably little in the way of release, it is not really surprising when he becomes less than keen on working in there.

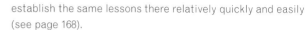

Working in the arena

As in everything you do with your horse, your first priority when working in the arena is to have him attentive and calm. Your next is to have him responding softly to everything you ask. Only then should you be concerned about where in the arena you are travelling, performing school figures and movements accurately, or teaching him something new (see pages 150–151).

Do not be in a rush to move up through the gaits. Teach and then establish what you want in walk first. Generally, if your horse is unsettled and braced in walk, he will only become more so as the speed increases. Conversely, if all is going well in walk, you should be able to move up through the gaits and

establish the same lessons there relatively quickly and easily (see page 168).

In itself, simply riding round and round an arena is of little value. As with groundwork, think instead of riding in the arena as an opportunity to:

• Develop your communication with your horse.
• Give him focus by being precise in what you ask – having a 'job' to do, however simple it may be, makes a big difference to a horse's motivation.
• Teach him specific things you want him to know.
• Develop him physically – and help keep him sound – so that he is able to do everything you want him to do better and better (see pages 165–167).

1) The ex-racehorse (see page 135) is tense and bracey as he moves from halt to walk...

2) ...walk to trot...

3) ...back down to halt...

4) ...and into rein back.

Is my horse bored?

All this is very different from assuming that your horse will get bored in an arena and that you therefore need to do lots of different 'things' with him. If your horse does something well, certainly it is a good idea to move on to something else, give him a break or even end the session right there. However, working through something with which your horse is struggling until he reaches an understanding will not 'bore' him, even if it takes some time, as long as you are clear and consistent in applying and releasing your cues. Your horse will then engage with the process, concentrate on what you are asking of him, keep trying to find the answer and feel good about the whole situation when he does.

Confusing and inconsistent riding is what makes horses 'bored' and fed up. They cannot make any sense of what is going on, and many will then simply 'switch off' and cease trying (others may react more dramatically – see page 180). Doing lots of different things with your horse in the arena is fine, as long as you follow each one through to the point where the horse understands what has taken place. Doing a bit of this and a bit of that but leaving each different thing in something of a muddle is extremely de-motivating to your horse.

Transitions

Transitions include not just changes of gait, but also of speed within the gait, of stride length and of direction. As when lungeing, long-lining or loose schooling your horse (see pages 113–124), it is a good idea to incorporate plenty of all these when riding in an arena, in order to:
• Keep up the flow of communication between you and your horse.
• Encourage him to keep concentrating, as he waits for your next instruction.
• Cause him to make little shifts of balance as he prepares for and executes each transition, thereby helping him to develop physically over a period of time.

6

5) Unsurprisingly, in canter he is even more tense and worried.

6) Reschooling the horse to relax and respond softly to the rider's requests needs to start here, in walk.

MOUNTING AND STANDING STILL

Mounting, and any other situation that requires the horse to stand still for a length of time, is often glossed over during training. Once in the saddle, many riders seem to forget how they struggled to get there, as the horse swung his hindquarters away from the mounting block for the umpteenth time or set off smartly as soon as they were halfway on.

Why doesn't my horse stand still for mounting?

There are a number of reasons why a horse may behave in this way, including:

• He is uncomfortable in his back and/or has a poorly fitting saddle (see pages 82–85). These issues should be resolved before a training solution is sought.
• The horse is not balanced over all four legs when the rider goes to mount, so he has to move to adjust to the weight.
• He has never been taught that standing still is what is required, so thinks that moving is correct (see box below).
• Being ridden is a confusing experience for him, so he tries to avoid it by making it difficult for the rider to mount.

Can my horse stand still at all?

Many horses cannot manage to stand still for more than a few seconds even when mounting is not involved. Often this is because there is never a time when people are around that *nothing* is happening – we are always doing something with, to or on them. If you want your horse to stand still for mounting (or for any other reason), you will need to take the time to teach him to do this.

When you are on the ground, a good cue for your horse to stand still and do nothing is that you do the same (this can be surprisingly difficult for some of us!). Do not hold him in place – the lead rope should be slack. If he moves, use the lead rope or body language to put him back where he was (see pages 100–102 and 108). Try to catch this early: between his thought and the action. Gradually build up the time for which you ask your horse to keep his feet still, do nothing and relax.

Most horses grow to enjoy just 'hanging out' with their handler in this way. Take any opportunity that presents itself to ask your horse to do nothing for a few minutes: it's excellent training for when you really need it.

How to teach a horse *not* to stand for mounting

• Assume that somehow the horse instinctively understands what is required, so neglect to teach him in a logical way what he should do.
• Dig him in the ribs with your toe as you go to mount, so that he moves forward in response.
• Each time he walks past the mounting block, swings his hindquarters away, swishes his tail or cow kicks as you go to mount – stop trying to mount, slacken the reins and/or take him away from the block, circling around to try again. Any or all of these actions reward the horse for behaviours you don't want, so he will repeat them. After just a few repetitions, a pattern will be set that he believes to be correct.

1) This horse is reluctant to move to the mounting block. It may be that he has never learned to lead from the bridle – many horses do not make the connection between this and leading from a headcollar unless taught – or that he is worried about standing near the block, or that he simply sees no reason to do so (in which case the basics of the relationship need some attention).

2) The rider gets him roughly into position, but he is still 'doing his own thing', rather than standing quietly and preparing to take the rider's weight.

Standing still for mounting

1) To teach the horse what is required, first the rider leads him step by step to the mounting block, so that he is lined up parallel to it. Once he has got the idea of this over several repetitions, she will be able to stand on the mounting block and guide him to it, but for now it is easier and more effective to guide him from the ground.

2) The rider checks the girth and then pulls on the stirrup leather so that the horse reorganizes his legs and widens his base of support, ready to take her weight. If he misses out this stage, he may lose his balance as she mounts and be forced to move his feet to regain it.

3) The rider places her foot in the stirrup and the horse stands well. This stage would be easier for both of them if he had been positioned closer to the block, but is a good first attempt.

4) The rider takes care not to poke her toe into the horse's belly or land heavily in the saddle, and again he stands still.

5) The rider sits still for a few moments so that she does not inadvertently ask the horse to move, then finds her right stirrup and organizes her reins. The horse has stood well throughout, and the rider will cue him to move off once she is ready.

3) As the rider gets ready to lift her foot to the stirrup, the horse steps away. He may do this for any of the reasons listed, or perhaps because he is used to being mounted while on the move...

4) ...which is exactly what happens next, confirming his actions as correct.

5) The horse then sets off with the rider still half on – potentially a very dangerous situation.

Standing still in other situations

Many horses find it difficult to stand still for a length of time in any ridden situation. Common scenarios include:

• The rider does not release the halt cue when the horse stops and stands still, so the horse continues to move in the hope of finding a release.

• The rider does not believe the horse can stand still without being held there with bit pressure. Many horses react to this by pulling the reins from the rider's hands as soon as they come to a stop in order to give themselves a release.

• Other horses in this situation will stand still while held by pressure on the bit, but move off as soon as it is released. They

1) The rider has asked the mare to halt but she has carried on moving forward. The rider picks up one rein and brings the horse's head around to the side.

2) With this much bend in her neck, the horse has to bring her forehand around and step across with her hindquarters. The rider does not use her legs at all to turn the horse – it must be the horse's choice to keep moving (or stop). In addition, the mare herself is already providing more energy than required, so there is no need for the rider to add in any more.

3) Eventually, after several revolutions, the mare stops her feet. The rider can now release the rein and allow the horse's neck to straighten, rewarding her for a correct response.

4) On the next attempt, the rider asks for halt and the horse stiffens and raises her head. The rider immediately lifts her hand to indicate to the horse that she is about to shorten the rein and bring her head around to the side, as before.

5) The horse doesn't stop moving, but she is already thinking about her response and her feet have slowed. The rider shortens one rein...

6) ...and after barely a quarter turn, the mare stops her feet.

have learned that constant pressure is the cue for stand still and are prepared to put up with it – these are generally the less reactive types. They have also learned that the release of bit pressure means move off and think they are responding correctly.
• The horse is tense and anxious, and his rider has not shown him an alternative, more beneficial way of being.

Teaching your horse to stand still *himself*

In order for your horse to learn to stand still quietly for as long as you require without being held there or yanking the reins from your hands, you need to help him reach the decision that this is his best option.

Start by riding your horse from walk to halt, and when he stops moving, release your cue to reward him for the correct response.

He will probably move off again, either instantly or after a couple of seconds. Immediately ask him to halt, and if he does not, pick up one rein (allowing the other to go slack) and bring his head around to that side. When his head is far enough around, he will be compelled to start moving his back end in the other direction. This has two effects:
1) You have disengaged his back end from his front, so there is no longer any power from his hindquarters to propel him forwards.
2) You have not punished him for moving or forced him to stop, but instead you have given him a choice: continue moving, but in this tight little 'circular' motion where the hind end moves around the forehand, or stop.

Eventually – and with some horses it can take a little time – you will feel the horse's hind end prepare to stop moving. At this moment (or, if you miss it, when he actually stops), release the rein and let his head and neck straighten. This is his reward for the correct response. Sit quietly yourself: you do not want to ask him to move by mistake!

Each time your horse moves without you asking him to, your response should be the same (but change the side to which you turn his head from time to time). Eventually, he will understand what you want and also that *it is the easiest thing for him to do*.

Once your horse is stopping and standing consistently, you can ask him to soften to the bit as he halts (see pages 144–147). If you try to do this earlier, he may become confused, as at that stage he needs an instant release to tell him that stopping and standing still is the response you are after.

Inside and out

A horse that has learned the benefits of standing still in this way will not just be keeping his feet still: his mind and emotions, his 'inside', will be quiet as well. In short, he will be happy to stop and stand still for as long as you like because it *feels good to him to do so*. A horse that has not discovered this may be standing still, but his mind and emotions are still in motion – he is only standing still on the 'outside', and as soon as he can, he will begin moving physically as well.

△ **On the next attempt, the mare halts instantly with no further help from the rider. She even drops her head and softens to the bit.**

One rein again

If your horse has learned to pull the reins through your hands when he stops, he may continue to do this even when he receives a release for stopping and standing still. He is so busy repeating his habitual behaviour that he probably hasn't noticed!

To change this pattern, stop your horse and release the rein when he does so without letting it right out (see box on page 144). Place one hand on your horse's withers or the front of the saddle and hold the rein firmly without changing its length or putting any pressure on your horse's mouth. When the horse pushes down with his head, he will instantly come up against this rein (the other rein can run through your hand) and his head will turn – you do not need to do anything yourself. This is effective because:
1) The horse cannot brace his neck against one rein as he can against two, so he is unable give himself a release by pulling the reins out of your hands (or your seat out of the saddle).
2) The horse brings *himself* up against the rein by pushing his head down and teaches *himself* that this is not the best option – the timing of the pressure and release are perfect, as human error has been taken out of the equation!

After a number of repetitions (change the hand you fix from time to time), your horse will realize that it is easier and more comfortable *not* to push down on the bit in this way, and that in any case he has already been given a release for stopping and standing still.

HOW YOUR HORSE MOVES

As we saw in Chapter 3, it's not just important *that* your horse does what you ask, it's also important *how* he does it. Now that you are on board, your weight on his back will affect your horse's balance and movement. In addition, he can no longer see your cues, body language, energy and focus – he has to *feel* them and discover how to respond.

Softness

There are a number of reasons why it is important to find and develop softness in your horse, and we have already looked at some ways of working on this from the ground (see pages 109–112). You now need to show your horse that his response to a cue from your hand or leg should be to soften, not brace against it. Once again, it is essential that you *always* release when your horse softens and *never* release when he braces.

How much release?

Releasing your reins when your horse softens to the bit does not necessarily mean dropping them entirely or even putting huge amounts of slack into them (although it can do): a horse can also feel it if you simply soften your fingers a little more on the reins.

Different amounts of release are appropriate for different horses at different stages of their training, and a good instructor will be able to help you with making these sorts of decisions.

Equally, a horse can feel it when you first start to pick up reins that are completely loose, just as well as he can feel a light contact on the reins become stronger. The question is whether he understands what this means and how he should respond – this is what working on softness is all about. Again, different amounts of 'pressure' are appropriate for different horses at different stages of their training.

If you find it hard to believe that a horse can discern such subtle changes in the feel on the reins, try the same thing with a set of reins and a human partner (with eyes closed) using their hands to feel what you are doing – and the horse is doing this through a bit placed in his sensitive mouth!

On the way to collection

In Chapter 3 we worked on softness through backing up (see pages 110–111), aiming for the horse first to release the muscles of his whole topline, then to raise his back and use his abdominal muscles and hindquarters to carry himself – in this case, backwards – smoothly and effortlessly. This is 'collection' and is the way a horse needs to use his body in order to carry a rider easily and efficiently over many years of work without incurring physical damage. It also feels wonderful to ride a horse that is operating in this way!

It is important to note that this is *not* the same as the horse being ridden constantly 'in a frame' (some riders call this 'on the bit'):
- The horse does not have to be in a frame in order to collect.
- The horse does have to be soft in order to collect.
- The horse can be in a frame and be neither soft nor collected.

For more about collection, see pages 165–167.

Working on softness

There are several simple ways you can begin to ask your horse for softness from the saddle. If you have worked on softness from the ground using a headcollar only (see pages 110–112), you will probably find that your horse does not recognize pressure from the bit as being the same request. However, because the groundwork you have done will have established soft responses to a variety of 'pressures', he will be likely to choose this response more quickly when he first encounters pressure on the bit.

▷ The ex-racehorse (see pages 135 and 138–139) has not yet learned how to soften his jaw and reach out to the bit, so in response to light pressure on the rein he tucks in his nose, scrunches up his neck and 'breaks' at the third vertebra (note the sharp angle at the highest point of his neck). This action does nothing to release the muscles of his topline, and he is still bracing hard.

SOFTENING TO ONE REIN

1) The rider has asked the horse to give softly to a feel on the right rein, and the horse has not only flexed nicely to the side but also lowered her head as the muscles along the top of her neck relax.

2) The rider has asked for a little more and the horse has brought her head further around. Note that when viewed from the front the horse's face is still vertical. This is far enough, because…

3) …bringing the horse's head around even further has caused her to tip her nose up so that her face is no longer vertical. This is because she is now using a different joint in her neck to bend around further, without releasing the neck muscles as desired.

SOFTENING TO TWO REINS

Softness – every time

The bottom line is that whenever you pick up your reins, your horse should soften to the bit rather than brace against it.

1) The rider picks up her reins and puts light pressure on the bit, and the horse responds by…

2) …relaxing her jaw and releasing the muscles along the top of her neck so that the topline appears to lengthen. These actions give her instant reward by putting a little slack in the reins.

1) This horse is learning to soften to the bit while on the move. The rider has picked up a light feel on the reins and the mare has braced her jaw and neck in response.

2) The rider maintains the same light pressure on the horse's mouth and she eventually softens her jaw and neck, giving herself the reward of an instant release as her actions put a little slack in the reins.

A hard mouth?

When a rider feels their horse habitually pushing against the bit, they often assume that the horse has a 'hard mouth'. In fact, almost always what they are feeling is the horse bracing his muscles as a learned response to pressure on the bit. Unlike a 'hard mouth', which implies physical damage that cannot be undone, a learned response can be unlearned and replaced with something else – softness. With some horses, who have learned their original lesson well and over many years, it may take some time and persistence to persuade them that a better option is available!

1) The rider asks the mare to back up and she starts to move her feet, but she is bracing her jaw and neck against the rein. The rest of her body is stiff and hollow, so her steps are small and shuffling.

2) Now the mare is starting to soften through her body, using her abdominal muscles to round up and carry herself and her rider backwards.

3) As the horse softens further, her steps become longer and more fluid. It feels to the rider as if backing up is no effort for either her or the horse.

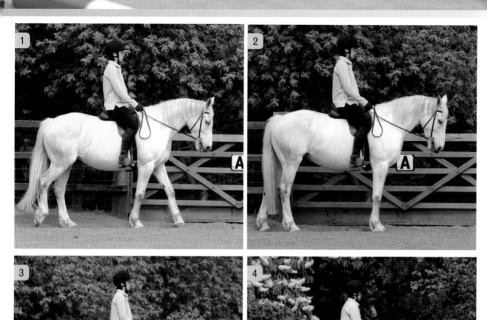

1) This horse moves softly from walk…

2) …into halt…

3) …and back up into walk.

4) She then maintains softness as she moves on up into trot.

The perils of pulling

If you want your horse to respond softly when you pick up your reins, it is important that you don't pull. Many of us do this without realizing, and it makes a big difference to the horse. To test whether you are pulling, take a set of reins and a helper, who will be the 'horse' while you are the 'rider':

1) Face each other, each of you holding a rein in each hand.

2) Pick up a little pressure on your reins, as you would when asking your horse to soften to the bit.

3) Your helper now tightens their hands against the pressure and perhaps moves them around, as your horse might brace and move his head and neck around. Do not watch their hands.

4) At some point, your helper should soften their hands, just as the horse will at some point offer to soften to the bit. Now check what your hands do in response:

  • Do they remain gently in place as you feel your helper's hands soften, allowing you to soften your fingers instantly as a release? This is what you want.

  • Do they move, even jerk, back towards you as your helper's hands soften, so that you miss the moment and cannot offer an instant release? You are pulling. This means that as your horse gives (softens), you take (carry on pulling) rather than give back (soften). Your horse will find it extremely difficult to work out the correct response in this situation. 'Fiddling' with the reins and/or holding them with stiff, tense arms and hands can have similar consequences.

Now swap with your helper, so that you are the 'horse' and they the 'rider'. It can be very instructive to put yourself in your horse's place.

1) This mare is distracted and paying no attention to her rider. She is tense and braced, and moving with her back hollow and hindlegs trailing out behind her.

2) The rider needs to re-establish softness. She picks up one rein to bring the mare's head and neck around, allowing the other to slacken as she does so. She also uses her inside leg to ask the mare to step her hindleg well underneath her body.

3) This back view shows the manoeuvre – sometimes called a 'loose turn on the forehand', as the forelegs keep moving – very clearly. As the mare steps her hindleg under and across, the topline muscles over her loins and hindquarters release.

4) As the horse moves out of the turn, the physical relaxing effects can be seen in her soft, rounded back and hindquarters. The mental effects are clear from the change in her demeanour. This movement can be performed from halt or walk.

SOFTENING IN TURNS

When you ask your horse to turn, softness should be your first priority. If he makes the turn but is still bracing against the rein, keep your cue in place until he 'lets go'. Only when he responds softly through his whole body every time you ask him to turn should you be concerned about where you end up going!

1) As she enters a left turn, the mare looks relatively soft and attentive...

2) ...but as the rider asks her to bend she braces against the rein.

3) As the turn progresses, the mare becomes stiffer and more braced instead of softer.

4) At the next attempt, the mare again begins by bracing her jaw and neck...

5) ...but the rider maintains the light pressure on the rein, and she starts to soften...

6) ...and then 'lets go'. She will now be able to soften and bend her body through the turn.

Straightness

Straightness in a moving horse is a prerequisite for collection, but it cannot be forced.

• To start, your horse needs to be attentive, calm and soft.

• Once he is soft, he can become supple. Some horses with the necessary physical attributes are naturally quite supple – these are the ones that offer some degree of collection almost from the word go. Others require more help to develop their suppleness.

• A soft, supple horse is able to move straight. If your horse cannot move straight, he cannot *freely* round himself up.

• Once your horse moves soft and straight he will begin to collect *himself*. With nothing blocking the power coming through from his hindquarters, impulsion follows naturally.

It should be clear that you cannot 'create' impulsion (or rounding up, or straightness) in a horse that travels crookedly by driving him forward – let alone into a strong hand – without causing tension, stiffness and bracing (see page 165).

1) The horse is bending nicely on a circle: his inside hindleg steps underneath his navel, his rib cage is swinging more to the outside than the inside, his shoulders are upright and there is a soft bend in his neck.

2) At the 'opposite' moment in the stride, the picture is just the same.

3) In another part of the arena, the horse finds it more difficult to bend. His inside hindleg steps almost in the track of the foreleg and his neck is straight.

4) At this point the horse is almost bending his head and neck to the outside and is leaning his shoulders inwards. He looks more as if he is moving on a straight line than on a circle. It is common for horses to set up patterns in which they can be softer in some areas of the arena than others, and you can use this to your advantage by teaching the horse what you want in a place where he finds it easier, then moving to a more difficult area once the idea is well established.

ONE CUE, ONE ACTION

At its simplest, riding involves applying a cue that your horse understands and him responding by organizing his body and performing that action. You will confuse your horse if you use the same cue for different actions, or different cues for the same action.

Teaching your horse something new from the saddle follows exactly the same principles as when you are on the ground, and your horse learns in exactly the same way.

A simple example: turn on the forehand

1) To begin teaching turn on the forehand, the rider flexes the horse's head slightly to the right and exaggerates the cue for the mare to step over behind by taking her right leg way back.

2) The horse does not respond, so the rider chooses to increase the bend in the neck as a secondary cue that will cause the mare to step her hindleg over.

3) The horse either misunderstands the leg as a cue to move forward or takes the physically easier option. Because the mare has not yet come up with the desired response, the rider keeps her right leg in position and will only release it when the mare steps over behind. She does not increase the pressure from her leg but simply waits for the mare to find the solution.

4) The mare stops and begins to step her hindleg over. The rider is already releasing the leg cue, allowing her leg to drop back into a normal position. The earlier she can release the cue, the clearer it is to the horse that she is on the right track with her response and the quicker she will learn.

5) At the next attempt, the rider does not need to put nearly so much bend in the horse's neck before she responds to the leg cue by stepping over behind…

6) …and the next step requires even less bend.

7) The mare now understands what is required, and the rider can dispense with the exaggerated leg cue as well. From now on, a small flex in the neck and light leg cue applied slightly further back than normal will produce the desired step. The rider can build from here to asking the horse for several steps at a time.

Multiple cues?

With horses (and humans), it generally pays to keep things simple. 'One cue, one action' is therefore a useful rule of thumb. Bombarding your horse with multiple cues for a single action can lead to confusion and resentment: a click of the rider's tongue, nudge with a leg, push with the seat and tap with a stick, for example, is a lot for a horse to decipher in one go. Reasons why riders do this might include:

• Disbelief that the horse will willingly respond to a single cue that he understands, and must therefore be *made* to perform by the rider using physical means.

• The horse has become confused and resentful, and largely switched off to the rider's requests, so many cues are needed to produce enough motivation for him to respond.

• The rider has not considered the possibility that the horse is in fact responding to just one of the cues they are giving. Trying these separately should identify the one that is actually working. Using just that cue in future will be a lot less hassle for both horse and rider.

• With a particularly sensitive horse, the rider's initial cue – a nudge with the leg, say – may have caused him to pin his ears and swish his tail without offering the required action. The rider then quickly adds in several more cues in an effort to get the horse to perform (in effect, increasing the pressure). The horse either repeats his previous response but more forcefully, or performs the required action but in a somewhat more extreme form! Going back and *reducing* the original cue – to, say, a light brush of the leg – rather than increasing it may produce the desired result.

Helping your horse

A cue is a signal that tells your horse *what* you want him to do. Your body position, small shifts of weight, energy, focus, breathing and so on are additional aids that help your horse understand *how* you want him to do it, by having a direct effect on *his* body position, weight distribution, energy, focus and breathing.

Your horse needs to learn the 'what' before he learns the 'how': once your horse can reliably produce the action you want in response to a specific cue, you can then shape that action to produce, say, more bend, slower steps, increased softness and so on. A good instructor will be able to help you with this as you and your horse progress.

Refining communication: beyond cues

Ultimately, once you and your horse have built up a really good level of communication, you may be able to reduce your cues to the point where your horse appears almost to respond to your thoughts and intentions alone. This may sound a bit mystical, but it's actually not: what you think affects your body in small ways that you may not notice, but your horse will.

However, be prepared to return to the cues your horse understands at any time if he stops responding or seems to be getting confused. You can always fade them out again once you are both back on track.

TIMING YOUR CUES

To keep your horse working happily, it is important to time your cues accurately. Apply a cue at the moment in your horse's stride when it is easy for him to respond and he will be able to carry out your request softly, willingly and promptly; apply it at any other time and his response may be delayed and full of tension.

In order to apply a particular cue at exactly the right time, you will first need to understand how your horse moves and then learn to feel where each of his feet is at any given moment.

Sequence of the horse's steps

- **Walk** – left hind, left fore, right hind, right fore (four-beat gait).
- **Trot** – left hind and right fore together, right hind and left fore together (two-beat gait).
- **Canter (right lead)** – left hind, right hind and left fore together, right fore (three-beat gait).
- **Canter (left lead)** – right hind, left hind and right fore together, left fore (three-beat gait).

In both trot and canter there is also a moment of suspension when all four feet are off the ground. It is important to be aware of this, particularly in canter, as this is the moment when the horse can rearrange his legs to make a change of lead.

1) At this moment in the stride, the horse's left hindleg is about to leave the ground. The barrel has swung out to the left and the rider's left leg has been pushed out with it. Her left foot is now higher than her right, and her left hip and seatbone have also been pushed up.

2) The left hindleg is now in the air and the two sides of the rider are almost level. The horse's barrel is just beginning to swing out to the right.

3) The horse's left hindleg has stepped down and the right hindleg is about to leave the ground. The barrel has swung out to the right and the rider's right leg has been pushed out with it. Her right foot is now higher than her left, and her right hip and seatbone have also been pushed up.

Feeling the feet

As your horse moves, the barrel of his body swings out first to one side and then the other, in order to create the space for his legs to move underneath him. This is the case in every gait. There is also forward movement, alternately on each side of the horse's body, which becomes more marked at faster gaits. These observations provide an easy way for the rider to feel what the horse's feet are doing at any time. There are several options:

• Feel your legs being swung first to the left as your horse's barrel swings left, and then to the right as the barrel swings right.
• Feel your left seatbone being pushed up as your horse's barrel swings left, and your right seatbone being pushed up as the barrel swings right.
• Feel your left hip being pushed up as your horse's barrel swings left, and your right hip being pushed up as the barrel swings right.
• Feel your left shoulder moving back as the horse's left shoulder moves back, and your right shoulder moving back as his right shoulder moves back.

Once you can feel these movements (and you cannot do this unless you are moving with your horse – see page 132), you can match the feeling with the movement of your horse's feet.

• **Hind feet** When the horse's barrel has swung as far as it can to the right, the right hind foot is about to leave the ground. As the horse lifts this leg and begins to move it forward, the barrel begins to swing to the left to get out of the way. When the right hind is underneath the horse, about to set on the ground, the barrel is out to the left. When the horse's barrel has swung as far as it can to the left, the left hind foot is about to leave the ground.

• **Front feet** When the horse's barrel has swung as far as it can to the left, the right fore foot is about to leave the ground. When the horse's barrel has swung as far as it can to the right, the left fore foot is about to leave the ground. When the horse's left shoulder has swung as far back as it can, the left fore is about to leave the ground. When the horse's right shoulder has swung as far back as it can, the right fore is about to leave the ground.

1) At this moment in the stride, the horse's right foreleg is about to leave the ground. The barrel has swung out to the left and the rider's left leg has been pushed out with it. Her left foot is now higher than her right, and her left hip and seatbone have also been pushed up.

2) The horse's right foreleg has stepped down and the left foreleg is about to leave the ground. The barrel has swung out to the right and the rider's right leg has been pushed out with it. Her right foot is now higher than her left, and her right hip and seatbone have also been pushed up.

Influencing barrel swing

Because the horse's barrel must swing from side to side when he is in motion, anything the rider does that interferes with this natural movement or prevents it from happening will either slow him down or stop him moving altogether.

This knowledge can be used to your advantage: deliberately stop your legs swinging with the swing of the horse's barrel or even tighten your thighs slightly around him, and you have a powerful aid for slowing or stopping.

It can also work against you: apply a prolonged squeeze with both calves (as many riders do) to ask your horse for forward motion and you may actually block the movement you have requested. Any tension in the rider's legs may also reduce the horse's ability to move forward freely.

Choosing the moment

Whatever gait he is performing, each of your horse's feet will spend a period of time in contact with the ground (known as the 'stance phase') and a period of time travelling through the air ('swing phase').

When your horse's foot is on the ground, it is committed to that step. If you cue a particular foot at this moment in the stride, your horse will either have to delay his response or contort his natural movement in some way in order to comply. Once the foot leaves the ground, however, the horse can move it faster or slower, more or less powerfully, or in a different direction, with ease.

The moment to apply a cue to influence a particular foot is therefore just as it is about to leave the ground, which gives the horse maximum time to produce the change.

Example 1: canter strike-off

In canter on the left lead, it is the right hind that initiates the first step of canter. Time your

cue to influence this foot to strike off into canter by applying it when the horse's barrel has swung out as far as it can to the right, which is when the right hind foot is about to leave the ground. Reverse this timing for canter on the right lead.

Example 2: leg yield

In leg yield to the left, the right hind leg must step across in front of the left to produce the sideways movement. Time your cue to influence this foot to step over by applying it when the horse's barrel has swung out as far as it can to the right, which is when the right hind foot is about to leave the ground. Release the cue as the horse steps his right leg across and reapply it when the right hind foot is next about to leave the ground to ask for another step of leg yield. (If you leave your cue on throughout, you will hinder the movement of the horse's barrel and lose both impulsion and the sideways movement that you want.) Reverse this timing for leg yield to the right.

1) The rider is asking the horse to leg yield to the right, using her left leg to cue the horse's left hind to step further across underneath him. This is the moment in the stride to apply the cue: just as the left hind is about to leave the ground. The horse's barrel has swung out to the left and the rider can feel this – her left leg has swung out too, and her left seatbone and hip have been pushed up (note the difference in the level of her stirrups).

2) As the horse lifts his left hind foot from the ground, his barrel begins to swing to the right – the rider's stirrups are now on a level...

3) ...and as the horse steps across his barrel swings further to the right, the rider's left leg swings with it, her left hip and seatbone begin to drop, and her left stirrup is now slightly lower than her right. She has already released her leg cue.

4) The horse is about to place his left hind foot on the ground and the rider's left side has dropped even further. Applying a leg cue at this moment in the stride, or...

5) ...even when the horse's left hind foot is firmly planted on the ground, will be counterproductive since he cannot move it. The horse's barrel is now out to the right – note the position of the rider's left hip, seatbone and leg.

5

4

1) The rider wants to make a transition from trot into canter on the left lead. The horse's right hind leg will initiate the first step of canter and this is the moment to cue it to do so – when it is just about to leave the ground.

2) In response to the cue, the right hind leg is stepping through with more energy…

3) …and the horse strikes off easily into canter.

Example 3: simple turn

To initiate a left turn, the horse's left foreleg must step out to the left and away from his body. Time your cue to influence his left foot by applying it when the horse's barrel has swung out as far as it can to the right (this is also when his left shoulder has swung as far back as it can), which is when the left fore foot is just about to leave the ground. Reverse this timing to initiate a right turn.

All movements and gaits you want from your horse can be achieved in the same way as in these examples – by working out which foot you need to influence, feeling when it is about to leave the ground and applying your cue at that moment.

1) The horse's movements have been deliberately slowed and the turns exaggerated for clarity in these photographs, so do not expect observations of your own horse to be as clear cut. Here the rider is looking to turn right, but this is the wrong moment to cue the mare to do so: her right foreleg is anchored on the ground while the left foreleg is about to lift up and take the next step. To turn right, the horse would have to delay for one step...
2) ...or cross her left foreleg awkwardly in front of her right.
3) This is the correct moment to cue for a turn to the right: the horse's right foreleg is about to leave the ground...
4) ...and can step out easily to the right to initiate the turn.

TOO FAST, TOO SLOW

Many horses choose the speed at which they move when ridden. This may vary from moment to moment, even from completely 'asleep' to running flat out in a matter of seconds! It may also vary in different situations: many horses go too fast for the rider when out hacking, only to switch off completely when in an arena.

Although you need to work with your horse's natural tempo rather than against it, it should still be you *not* the horse who selects the speed at which you both travel. Quite apart from anything else, safety is an issue if the horse is taking these sorts of decisions.

When you are able to set your horse's speed, and vary it at will, this will have a big effect on his understanding of how your relationship works. He will generally become much more relaxed, attentive and co-operative as a result. You are then ready to start hacking out again in far greater safety.

The fast horse

A horse may travel too fast for a number of reasons, including:
• The horse is suffering from physical discomfort of some kind, and in effect is running away from it (even in walk). This should be resolved before any training solutions are sought.
• The rider has never attempted to take charge *at all times* of the speed at which the horse travels in each gait.
• The rider is tense, causing tension in the horse, and vice versa.
• The horse is fearful and is, in effect, 'fleeing' from the situation (even in walk).
• The horse loses his balance (particularly in downward transitions) and takes more weight on his forehand, making it difficult for him to slow down even if he wanted to.

Most riders' instinctive reaction to their horse moving too fast is to try to shut off his excess energy, most often by using both reins in an attempt to slow him down or even stop him. Unfortunately, with a horse that feels he needs to be using that amount of energy, this approach usually makes the situation worse.

Taking the energy the horse is offering and directing it is generally more beneficial. It will slow the horse down and also explain to him in a way he understands that what he was doing was not what you wanted, *and* show him exactly what he should be doing instead.

To direct your fast horse's energy:
1) Immediately he takes the first step that is too fast, shorten one rein to bring his head around and allow the other rein to go slack, so that you direct your horse on to a fairly tight circle. Do not use your legs: there is enough energy in the system already!
2) Keep riding circles, figures of eight, serpentines and any other wiggly, non-straight paths you fancy as long as he is moving too fast. Each time you change direction, make sure the new outside rein becomes slack.
3) The moment you feel your horse offer a step at the (slower) speed you want, immediately allow him to go straight again.

Safety first

Be cautious about using this approach in canter: if your horse is cantering on, say, the left lead and you turn him tightly to the right, he may get his legs in a tangle and even fall. Even on the correct lead, turning in a tight curve could possibly result in a fall – although too large a circle may be ineffective.

Generally, it is better to get your horse working in a quiet, balanced way in walk and trot before moving up into canter, by which time you may find he no longer feels the need to rush. For more about cantering, see pages 168–170.

4) The moment he takes a faster step, move him on to a tight curve once more.
5) Continue in this way, responding as quickly and consistently to your horse's changes in speed as you can. Eventually, he will come to realize that you want him to move at the slower speed all the time.

This type of approach works for a number of reasons:
• Working in this way means the rider has to notice the speed at which the horse is moving *at every stride*.
• Using one rein effectively 'breaks' the brace in the horse's neck and body that he is using to push through two reins. Instantly, you are no longer fighting with your horse.
• Bringing his head and neck around as you put him on a tight curve disengages his back end from his front to some degree, so he cannot power forward. You now have control over your horse.
• Moving on a tight curve at speed is harder work for the horse. Relatively quickly, he will start to search for an easier way to go – and slowing down is an obvious option for him to try.

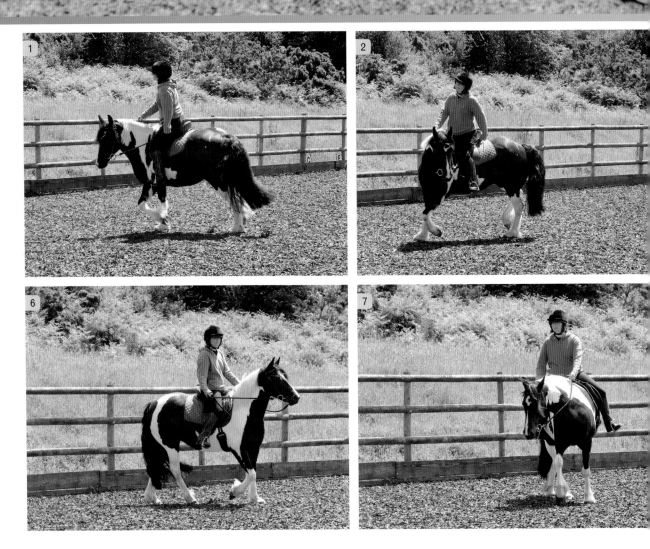

• While on the curve, the horse has to be more aware of where he is placing his feet and will need to find his balance (since he cannot just run forward as he could when on a straight line).

• The reward for a correct response is readily understood and appreciated by the horse: it is much easier for him to move in a straight line.

• Removing any element of forcing, fighting or punishment allows the horse to discover for himself what is his best option – and what horses teach themselves tends to stick.

The slow horse

A horse may travel too slowly for a number of reasons. These might include:

• The horse is suffering from physical discomfort of some kind and as a result finds it difficult to move freely. The horse's discomfort should be resolved before any training solutions are sought.

• The rider has never attempted to take charge *at all times* of the speed at which the horse travels in each gait.

• The rider is inadvertently blocking the horse's movement by not going with it (see page 132), tensing up, or using cues such as a strong squeeze with both legs or a forward push with the seat that opposes the side-to-side movement of the horse's barrel (see box on page 153).

• The horse has been trained to ignore the rider's cues (for example, through mis-timed releases, no release, inconsistency – see pages 134–135).

• The horse does not understand the cue to move faster: he believes that a kick every stride means keep going at the same speed, and when the kicking stops it means slow down.

Many riders react to this situation by trying to keep the horse going or speed him up through physical means – pushing with the seat, kicking, use of a stick or spurs – applied constantly and/or in

1) At the start of a schooling session, this mare is anxious at being in an arena she has not seen before and away from her friends in the stables. Instead of walking along quietly as requested, she tries to trot off at speed towards the gate, so the rider picks up one rein and brings the horse's head around to the side.

2) As she turns, the mare is still trotting and is bracing against the inside rein. Note that the rider is leaving slack in the outside rein.

3) As the mare gives to the inside rein, her feet are beginning to slow and her hindquarters are coming around, ready to line up with her front end.

4) The instant the mare drops into walk, the rider releases the inside rein and allows her to straighten up. The mare proceeds in walk, but is still a little tense and anxious.

5) A little later, working on the other rein, the mare again becomes distracted and tries to break into trot. The rider immediately picks up one rein, which the horse then braces against, and leaves slack in the other.

6) This time, the mare gives almost instantly to the pressure on the inside rein and drops her head as she returns to walk.

7) By the time they have returned to the rail, the horse is back to work and concentrating on the rider, not the surroundings.

a random fashion. The result is generally that the horse becomes less rather than more sensitive to the rider's cues.

It is less work and more pleasant for both parties to teach the horse the meaning of a light leg cue ('go faster') in a logical and unambiguous way, and then allow him to produce the extra energy himself, rather than to try to squeeze it out of him at every stride.

To teach your slow horse to speed up willingly:
1) Find a 'secondary cue' that you think will motivate your horse to move forward. This might be a stick, a soft rope, a leafy branch from the hedge – some horses have become desensitized to most items humans hold in their hands, so you may have to use your ingenuity.
2) As your horse sets off at his slow speed, ask him to speed up by using a light touch of your legs (or a click of your tongue, or whatever you choose) *once only*. This is your primary cue, the one to which you eventually want him to respond.

3) If there is no response, go to your secondary cue. Begin by flicking your stick (or whatever you have chosen) out to the side of your horse in a continuous rhythm. The instant your horse speeds up, stop the movement of the stick to reward him and simply allow him to carry you forward.
4) If your horse does not respond to the stick out to his side, move on to tapping the stick on your boot or the saddle, again in a continuous rhythm, until he does. If this is not enough to motivate your horse, move on to tapping him lightly in the same way.

1) The rider is asking this mare to move from walk to trot, but receives no response to her leg cue. Over time, the horse has become immune to it, and a stick has been used indiscriminately so that she has learned to ignore that as well. The rider therefore carries a soft rope to act as a secondary cue…

2) …and begins to lift it up and out, giving the horse the opportunity to respond to this signal to move into trot. However, the mare simply swishes her tail and braces her muscles, everything about her saying 'No way!'

3) As the rider swings the rope over the horse's withers, her reaction escalates into neck wringing and she lays back her ears. If the rider were to give up now, the horse would have learned to ignore yet another cue to move forward…

4) …so she perseveres, and the mare suddenly breaks into trot. The rider has left the reins slack, so that the horse can move freely forward.

5) As long as the mare continues to trot forward, the rider simply goes along with her. She does not use her leg to 'keep the horse going', and the rope remains inactive. If the horse tries to slow, the rider first touches her with her leg, and then if there is no response she starts to swing the rope.

6) The rider brings the horse back to walk and gives her a breather, then asks for trot again. Although she still has to back up her leg cue with the rope, this time she has just lifted it out and up and begun to swing it when the horse moves into a good trot. The mare looks altogether happier now.

7) On their third walk-to-trot transition, the rider has only to use her leg lightly and the mare moves off smartly into a ground-covering trot.

8) Back in walk, the mare's whole outlook has changed and her stride is much more willing and purposeful. She will need to be ridden in this way for some time, using the rope as (and only if) necessary to back up the leg cue, until she is responding absolutely consistently to just a light touch of the leg.

Speeding up the tapping will increase the 'pressure'. Be sure to stop tapping the instant he responds by speeding up.

5) When your horse does respond, he may only sustain the faster movement for a stride or two before dropping back to his habitual slower speed. *Every time* he does this, the moment you feel him take his first slower step go through the same routine again: primary cue, then secondary cue gradually increasing in intensity. Be sure to release your cue at whatever point in this routine your horse responds. Eventually – and with some horses it can take some time – your horse will learn that the primary cue means move faster (you can then drop the secondary cue) and that you want him to maintain this speed until you tell him to do otherwise.

This type of approach works for a number of reasons:

• Working in this way means the rider has to notice the speed at which the horse is moving *at every stride*.

• It uses a logical and consistent sequence of events to teach the horse the meaning of the cue for 'go faster'.

• Using tapping – instead of, say, one heavy kick or a smack with a stick – allows the cue to be applied continuously when the horse is not responding and stopped immediately he does.

• Unlike kicking at every stride or 'nagging', there is something in it for the horse when he finds the correct response: the cue ceases.

• By using a secondary cue, the horse can be re-sensitized to the primary cue.

• Removing any element of forcing, fighting or punishment allows the horse to discover for himself what is his best option – and what horses teach themselves tend to stick.

Feeling the moment

If you find it difficult to feel the instant when your horse takes his first slower (or faster) step, try counting the rhythm of the gait to yourself. This should help you to notice the moment at which the rhythm first slows down (or speeds up) and thereby improve the timing of your cues and releases.

Lessons to learn

Both the fast horse and the slow horse are good illustrations of how we often react instinctively to what horses do in a way that has totally the opposite effect to what we had intended. They also illustrate:

• The absolute importance of consistency when riding.
• The futility of fighting the horse.
• How horses can learn the exact opposite of what we think we are teaching, and then become wedded to patterns of behaviour.
• That these patterns can be changed, through retraining that makes sense to the horse.
• That, ultimately, as a rider you should aim to be aware (and in charge) of the quality of every step your horse takes.

Ride every step

Even if you do not have a problem with your horse moving too fast or too slow, it is a good idea to practise varying the speed within a gait – for example, from a fast, swinging walk to one where the horse is barely moving, and all stages in between. This involves increasing and decreasing the energy in your body, as well as cues; eventually, you may be able to suggest a faster speed to your horse just by increasing the power of your breathing, and a slower speed by using a softer, slower breath. Once the walk is so slow that you are communicating with your horse one step at a time, he will start learning to wait for your direction as to what to do with each step, even when the speed increases.

1) The rider is asking the horse to walk fairly fast, and she responds with a long, swinging stride.
2) The rider has now dropped the energy in her own body right down and picked up slightly on the reins, and the mare responds by slowing her walk until she is taking slow, short strides. She is now moving one step at a time, and listening intently to the rider to see exactly what she wants on the next step...

GETTING OUT OF YOUR HORSE'S WAY

Earlier, it was said 'Remember that in riding you are signalling to the horse what he is to do next and then *allowing him to do it*, not physically pushing and pulling him around' (see page 134). Many riders find this difficult to do, often because they do not believe the horse can learn a response, then willingly organize his own body to do the action and then do it. They feel they have to *make* him do it, from start to finish, otherwise he will choose to do something they would rather he didn't!

This belief is often the result of some degree of fear – the rider feels the need to keep 'control' – plus the experience of riding horses that have been trained and ridden in a physical push-and-pull way, so that all the rider's expectations are fulfilled every time they ride. However, this response is not the true nature of horses; in other words, it doesn't *have* to be this way.

Transitions

As a simple example, take a transition from trot to walk.

Common scenario:

• **Rider** applies the cue (say, rein pressure).

Horse begins to organize his body to make the transition.

• **Rider** continues to apply rein pressure.

Horse begins to make the transition.

• **Rider** continues to apply rein pressure.

Horse makes the first stride of walk.

• **Rider** continues to apply rein pressure.

Horse makes the second and third strides of walk.

• **Rider** finally releases the rein pressure.

Horse has been *made* to walk.

This lengthy process results in a slow transition where the horse almost grinds to a halt before setting off again in walk. The horse will also become dull to rein pressure because his first *three* responses were not rewarded with a release.

Alternative scenario:

• **Rider** applies the cue (say, rein pressure).

Horse begins to organize his body to make the transition.

• **Rider** releases the rein pressure.

Horse makes the transition to walk *himself*.

This results in a crisp transition where the horse flows easily from trot to walk and a horse that is responsive to rein pressure, because his efforts are rewarded instantly.

In order to make a transition like this, you will need to be able to feel the moment when the horse begins to organize himself

1) The rider has just asked to horse to transition from canter to trot, and at this moment everything looks on course…

2) …but as the horse tries to take his first step in trot we can see that she has used her hands way too strongly and almost pitched him on to his nose.

3) On the next step the rider has held on to the reins in an effort to prop up the horse, and he has virtually come to a halt as he tries to reorganize his body to move forward again.

4) As he does so, he is well out of balance and consequently his trot is heavy and lifeless.

5) At the next attempt, the canter looks similar – if a little better balanced – as the rider asks the horse to transition to trot.

6) This time, she has used her hands more lightly and released them earlier – the transition is smoother and the 'halt' has been eliminated.

7) This allows the horse to move forward into a powerful trot.

to change his movement from trot to walk. This takes both concentration and practice, but is well worth the effort for the improvement it will bring to the timing of your release and the quality of the transition.

When you first try this with a horse that is used to being made to walk (as in the common scenario overleaf), you may find that when you release your cue earlier he does not complete the transition to walk. This does not matter: simply ask again. You are in a process of training your horse to respond to the least cue possible, not getting him to walk at any cost. Remember: it is more important *how* your horse does something than *that* he does it.

You can help your horse to understand what is required by making sure you change your own body motion from 'trot' to 'walk' as you ask for the transition. (Many riders do this, but then add in a bit of 'halt' for good measure without realizing, which again produces a stop–start type of transition.) Eventually, you may want to refine your cue to just this change of motion in yourself, which by removing the 'interruption' of a cue such as rein pressure can help to smooth out the transition even further.

1) From this relaxed, soft canter…

2) …the rider asks the mare to transition to trot and she responds immediately by rebalancing, ready to make the change.

3) The rider allows the mare to make the transition to trot herself, and she does so softly and easily.

4) Within a couple of strides the rider asks the mare to walk, and again she complies softly and willingly to a light cue.

5) The rider then asks the mare to halt, and once again she does so easily. A quick succession of downward transitions like this requires light cues and well-timed releases if the horse's movement is to remain soft, fluid and forward throughout.

Collection

Collection provides another clear example of the importance of getting out of your horse's way.

What is collection?

Collection can be defined as a dynamic posture of the horse's spine that allows him to carry a rider over many years without compromising his soundness. It also looks and feels good to ride a horse that is using his body in this way.

The essential elements that allow a horse to collect himself are, first:

• Release of all the muscles of the topline.

Then:

• Coiling of the loins.
• Raising of the back.
• Raising of the base of the neck.

All three of these elements involve using the muscles of the underline instead.

When the rider tries to make the horse collect

For various reasons – one of the main ones being the perceived requirements of competition, as well as the fact that it looks and feels good – most riders would like their horse to carry himself with neck raised and arched, nose vertical, back rounded, quarters lowered and so on – and the horse would like to carry himself this way under his rider, if he knew it was an option (see page 166).

However, many riders try to *make* the horse adopt this posture, by pushing and pulling him with legs and hands, sometimes using 'training aids', and often with no release so that they are holding him in position, in order that he *looks* right in one or more of the desirable elements:

• Head down and nose vertical.
• Neck arched.
• Hindlegs moving further under him.
• More weight taken on the hind end.
• Frame shortened from front to back.

And so on. But these are the *effects* of collection, not the causes (see box left), and working in this way results in tension rather than release of muscles, stiffness and, over time, even physical problems and unsoundness. In other words, by the rider getting in the horse's way and trying to *make* collection happen, the outcome is poorer rather than better movement.

△ **This horse is displaying all the essential elements of collection, in a degree appropriate to the work he is performing. His lack of any tension or anxiety is obvious.**

△ **In contrast the muscles of this horse's topline are tight, his head is up, his neck is braced and the base of it dropped, his back is hollow, and most of his weight is on his forehand.**

1) As with the horse shown bottom right on page 167, this horse is tense and braced, his head is up and his back is hollow. The rider is keeping a contact on the reins in an effort to persuade the horse to drop his nose...

2) ... which he then tries to do – but the rider has maintained the contact and is now spurring him forward into it. The result is that the horse remains hollow, his neck is tense and pulled up and back as he continues to push into the bit, and his whole topline is braced. Driving the horse forward into a fixed hand will not teach him how to round up and carry himself in collection.

When the horse learns to collect himself

On page 147 we saw that if the horse is shown by the rider first how to be soft (release the muscles of his topline) and straight, he will then begin to round up *himself* and discover that this is a good way to carry a rider.

Over time, with training that focuses on softness, suppleness, straightness and balance, and that develops the strength of the muscles of the horse's underline, he will adopt increasing degrees of collection *himself* when required to do so by the rider and/or the activity in which they are engaged, without any accompanying increase in tension.

The horse will also begin to carry himself in some degree of collection at all times, even when just hacking along on a long rein, because he has found that this is the easiest way to go. Remember: collection is *not* the same as the horse being constantly 'in a frame' (see box on page 165, and page 144).

Circus act

Standing the horse's front feet on a 'circus drum' is an easy, fun way for the horse to experience what the posture of collection feels like.

△ This horse is carrying herself in relaxed collection. She may be just walking on a long rein, but all the essential elements are in place.

Strengthening the underline

Useful exercises to strengthen the muscles of your horse's underline over time include:
• Transitions of all kinds, including changes of gait, stride length and direction.
• Working correctly over poles.
• Backing up correctly – backing uphill is an even more powerful exercise.
Each of these involves the horse naturally increasing his degree of collection in order to carry out the manoeuvre. Pole work and backing uphill are quite strenuous for the horse, so should be built up slowly, starting from the ground and moving on to ridden work.

1) Trotting over poles – first on the lunge and then ridden – encourages the horse to use his body correctly. Before each pole he will momentarily increase his degree of collection, and practising this over time will help to strengthen his abdominal muscles. Using raised poles will increase the effort he has to make, so a few repetitions of the exercise in each session is plenty.

2) Unfortunately, trotting over poles 'upside down' is of no benefit at all. Many horses will do this once they have been down the same line of poles once or twice, so it is a good idea to change things around to keep the horse concentrating and collecting before each pole.

▷ Backing uphill is another good exercise to help the horse develop the muscles needed for collection. This mare is clearly using her hindquarters and abdominal muscles to carry herself back up the slope, with her back lifted and rounded. This is hard work, so build up the exercise a few steps at a time.

GOING FASTER AND LEAVING THE GROUND

Moving up through the gaits and increasing the speed tends to produce an increase in tension in the horse. In addition, any 'holes' in his training will show up more and more obviously as the speed increases.

Proper preparation

You can help your horse to accept faster speeds without an increase in anxiety by preparing him properly at slower gaits. Make sure attention, calmness and softness are well established at walk before moving into trot, and then at trot before moving into canter.

Do not be in a hurry to work at faster gaits. Tense work, with the horse most likely losing his balance and rushing as well, is of no value. If this way of going becomes established, you will then have to spend time retraining him (see pages 157–158).

Less is more

If your horse is worried about moving into a faster gait, a good way to help him is to ask for just a few good steps – there is no point in practising bad ones – and then come back to the slower gait, in which he feels comfortable. Then gradually build up the number of steps you ask for in the faster gait to build his confidence. Working in this way, you will probably find that it doesn't take long for him to feel comfortable in the new gait.

From the horse's point of view

Riders often assume that because the horse is fine in walk, he should be fine in trot and canter too, but to the horse this can feel like a whole new situation. Depending on a number of factors – the horse's experience, his temperament, the rider's anxieties and so on – he may or may not have to relearn what he knew well in walk once he moves into the faster gait. However, this should happen much more quickly than his initial learning in walk.

Cantering

Commonly, a horse and rider may do reasonably well in walk and trot, but fall apart when asked to make a transition to canter.

Two common problems

1) The horse shows tension or even bucks as he moves into canter. Reasons why a horse may do this include:
- **Restrictive saddle** The horse can just about cope in walk and trot, but not when he needs to move his shoulders more in canter. Find a saddle that works for your horse (see pages 82–85).
- **Physical discomfort** This should be resolved before any training solutions are sought.
- **Too strong a cue** Your idea of a light cue and your (very sensitive) horse's idea might not be the same! Try reducing your cue even further to see his response improves (see page 151).
- **Mis-timed cue** Applying your cue at the wrong time can upset a sensitive horse, so work on getting your timing right (see pages 152–156).
- **Anxiety about being in canter** Try the 'less is more' approach (above) to build your horse's confidence. Conversely, your horse may be so worried about cantering that he actually holds his breath as he makes the transition and does not take another breath for quite some time, or until he returns to trot. In this case, you will need to practise staying in canter long enough for your horse to start breathing in a regular fashion (you will be able to hear this quite clearly), when his anxiety level will drop.

2) The horse trots faster and faster, and may or may not eventually fall into canter.
Reasons why a horse may do this include:
- **Restrictive saddle** The horse's solution to being unable to move freely in canter is not to make the transition. Find a saddle that works for your horse (see pages 82–85).
- **Physical discomfort** This should be resolved before any training solutions are sought.
- **Loss of balance** The horse's weight falls more on his forehand as he speeds up, making it difficult for him to move into canter.
- **Confused cues** The rider uses the same cue for 'speed up' as for 'change from trot to canter'. The horse does not

1) This horse is already tense in trot as the rider urges him forward in anticipation of the transition to canter.

2) As the rider uses her legs strongly to ask for the transition, he tenses more, raises his head and speeds up his trot instead.

3) Finally he makes the transition, but the canter is bracey and tight.

1) Next time, the trot it is slightly less tense to begin with...

2) ... but as the rider asks for canter the horse again tightens up and rushes forward.

3) Instinctively, the rider leans forward, which actually makes it more difficult for the horse to push off into canter... but he manages it anyway, although he does not look particularly comfortable.

4) This time, the rider is able to cue the horse more quietly and move with rather than against him, and the whole picture is much more relaxed.

necessarily have to speed up in order to move from trot to canter – he just needs to change the sequence in which he moves his legs. Remember: one cue, one action (see pages 150–151).

• **Mis-timed cue** Even when the cue is distinct, applying it at the wrong time can upset a sensitive horse, so work on getting your timing right (see pages 152–156).

• **The rider stays in trot** As you ask for the transition and your horse organizes himself to begin cantering, if you do not change your own body motion to follow the canter instead of the trot, your horse may respond to this rather than your cue.

• **The rider doesn't feel confident about cantering** The horse feels the reluctance and tension in the rider's body, and perhaps a tighter feel on the reins, and responds accordingly by remaining in trot. If your horse is to commit to cantering, you need to as well. Find a good instructor who can help build your confidence.

1) From a soft, calm and attentive trot like this...

2) ...comes a canter transition like this.

Jumping

Jumping is not a particularly natural activity for horses – they will jump obstacles that are in their path, but usually prefer to go around them if possible. However, most horses are happy to jump for their riders as long as they understand what is required and how to do it, and are not asked to clear obstacles that are beyond their abilities.

Initially, horses may have a number of fears of jumping that arise from their nature as prey animals. For example:

• The appearance of the poles and jumps themselves may worry the horse, who is naturally suspicious of unusual-looking objects.

• When he begins to work over poles, the horse may worry about getting his feet trapped among them. A line of poles may appear innocuous enough to us, but to the horse – who needs to feel he can flee at a moment's notice – it can look like something to be avoided at all costs.

• Many horses become concerned when they hit a pole, especially if it rolls along the ground or falls from the jump. We know what is happening but the horse doesn't – an apparently inanimate object has suddenly come to life, and he is rightly suspicious as to what it might do next (especially as it is down there among his vulnerable legs and feet).

Careful and progressive training will usually overcome anxieties such as these relatively quickly.

Even once he is jumping well, a horse's confidence and enjoyment of jumping can be destroyed in a number of ways. These might include:

• **Restrictive saddle and/or physical discomfort** Jumping is a strenuous activity and may bring to light problems that were not apparent on the flat. These issues should be resolved before a training solution is sought.

• **Poor riding** The horse is inadvertently 'punished' every time he takes a jump by, for example, being pulled in the mouth or having the rider's weight thump down on his back as he lands.

• **Mismatched skill level** The rider is unable to help a green horse, or 'get out of the way' of a more experienced one.

• **Rider anxiety** The rider isn't confident to jump, causing the horse to lose confidence too or refuse to jump because he can feel that this is the rider's real intention. If you suspect that *you* are the problem, find a good instructor to help you improve your riding over jumps and build your confidence. You will then be in a position to help your horse.

• **Overfacing** Jumping large and/or difficult obstacles when a horse is too young or green will rapidly destroy his confidence.

• **Too much jumping** Jumping is hard work for a horse, and even if he knows he is able to do the job he may just become thoroughly fed up with the whole affair. Stop jumping, go back and reschool your horse from ground poles up. Progress slowly, and if it turns out that your horse has really had it with jumping, try to find him another job that he can enjoy.

◁ **Jumping natural obstacles while out hacking can help to maintain or rekindle your horse's enthusiasm for the job. This mare is confident both in her rider and in her own ability, and jumps a fallen tree with evident enjoyment.**

Two common problems

1) The horse refuses or runs out at the jump.

Many of the causes listed on pages 170–171 may be at the root of this problem. In addition, many riders mentally leave the situation and/or stop breathing a few strides from the jump, so that in effect the horse is 'on his own' and, quite reasonably, makes his own decision about what action to take. If this is your problem, now is the time when all your practice at staying present, breathing well and taking decisions for both of you (see pages 132–133) should pay off.

Take care, too, that you focus beyond the jump, on where you are headed next, rather than on the bottom of the fence – if your horse has learned to pay attention to your focus, he make take this literally!

2) The horse rushes as he approaches the jump.

Again, many of the causes listed on pages 170–171 may apply here as well. Contrary to popular opinion, a horse is more likely to race around a course of fences because he is anxious and therefore 'fleeing' than because he adores jumping. Rushing over jumps also appears to be more common with ponies, perhaps because children often urge them faster and faster in the hope that sheer speed will propel them over the jumps and prevent refusals. Agile ponies are able to do this, so they comply with their rider's request, until moving at high speed over jumps becomes an established pattern of behaviour that is reinforced by the pony's own adrenalin.

It is possible to work with a horse that is rushing over jumps in a similar way to one that is rushing on the flat (see pages 157–158). As soon as the horse takes a step on the approach to a jump that is too fast, turn him on to a curve away from the jump and continue working in this way until he offers the speed you want. Then approach the jump again and turn him away at his first fast step. You will find that this becomes closer and closer to the jump, until eventually – and it may take some time – the horse understands that you wish him to maintain the same, slower, speed all the way to the jump. If the horse then rushes away from the jump, you can work with him exactly as for the fast horse on the flat.

1) The rider is focusing well on the line she is riding, out beyond the jump, on the approach...

4) ...hangs in the air over the jump...

1-4) This mare competed at intermediate level eventing for several seasons before the stress overcame her and she became difficult, if not dangerous, to ride. Her rider stopped competing her for nearly three years, and patiently retrained her with softness as the overriding aim. The mare is now back eventing, with a totally different outlook – here she jumps a practice fence calmly and enthusiastically, and turns softly and easily for the next obstacle.

2) ...as the horse gathers to take off...

3) ...pushes off and up...

5) ...and lands. Riding the fence with such focus and intent throughout leaves no room for doubt in the horse's mind as to what is required and that his rider is there for him. This helps him to gain confidence in both himself and his rider.

RIDING OUT

Taking your horse out and away from his familiar surroundings, which include the arena, tends to produce an increase in tension. If your horse is not attentive, calm and soft in at least walk, trot, halt and backing-up at home, this will inevitably get worse once you are out and about, so it is only fair to him to make sure he is well prepared.

With a youngster, or if you know your horse has particular fears (such as plastic bags in the hedge, dogs or large vehicles), to start with work on these in the arena where you can control all the variables, progressing from in-hand and long-line work to riding (see pages 127–131).

△ **The arena – or a suitable field – is the safest place to work on getting your horse confident with traffic. Start with a small vehicle, stationary and with the engine switched off, and give the horse plenty of room. As he becomes comfortable with each stage, gradually increase the challenge: use larger vehicles, drive past the horse from both front and rear, and decrease the space through which he must pass by just a few inches at a time.**

Some common problems

The number one cause of most of the problems you are likely to encounter when riding your horse out and about is that the relationship and communication between you is not yet well enough established to keep him 'with' you when the situation becomes more challenging. The number one remedy for any problem is therefore to build a relationship in which the horse

looks to *you* when the chips are down, and this chapter and Chapter 3 are all about how to do this.

This is your long-term solution to the examples of common problems discussed next. It addresses the cause, rather than the symptom – the problem you are seeing – which then often disappears without having to be addressed directly. However, it is also worth looking at these situations from the horse's point

of view, in order to see if there are specific ways of helping him respond to them more positively. The suggestions given below are just that: suggestions, to get you thinking about ways in which you might approach problems you encounter with your horse from time to time. Bear in mind that prescriptive, 'quick-fix' answers may not necessarily be applicable to your particular horse's situation and rarely work long term.

If you feel you are out of your depth, or your horse's behaviour is becoming dangerous, you will need expert help. Do not attempt to deal with the problem yourself.

Becomes unruly in company

The horse is either excited or frightened. Whichever it is, and even if you believe he is or should be ready, *he* feels unprepared to deal with being ridden with a number of horses. Do not simply carry on riding him with a group in the hope that he will 'get used to it'. A better bet is to increase his exposure to other horses more gradually and to show him that he needs to continue to pay attention to you at all times.

• If your horse lives alone, or perhaps with just one other horse, try to introduce him to herd life. If the members of the herd change from time to time, this will help him get used to meeting other horses without becoming either over-excited or terrified (see page 59).

• Ride him out with one other, reliably quiet horse to start with. Enlist your friends' help to add one horse at a time, until he is able to cope with a group. Then swap the group members around regularly, until your horse is ready for anything.

• At all times, ride your horse exactly as you would in the arena or when hacking alone. Ask him to keep his attention on you, give him instructions to carry out, do not accept him taking the decisions about speed and direction, and so on.

1) Riding out with a steady companion will give your horse confidence in company. Here the chestnut is a little unsure, but follows the more experienced bay horse anyway.
2) After a little while his confidence grows and he is able to come up alongside.
3) Eventually, he is able to travel fast across open country alongside his companion without concern.

Refuses to be ridden out on his own

This problem often shows up when the horse is in company as well – he is very reluctant to take the lead in front of other horses, tries to tuck in directly behind, and takes his 'instructions' on speed and direction from the other horses rather than you. The basic cause is lack of confidence in his ability to cope and in yours to help him, so you will need to continue working on your relationship. In addition, poor training may have inadvertently rewarded the horse for taking his own decisions in this way.

• Check first that your horse is not in pain or being restricted in his movement by an ill-fitting saddle, as this will make him reluctant to move out freely. If he works well at home, this is unlikely to be a factor.

• Check that your horse *really* understands the cue to move forward: he should respond promptly to just *one* use of the cue, *every* time. If he does not, work on this at home before venturing out (see pages 158–161).

• Make absolutely sure you are not 'nagging' (see pages 158–161, and box on page 179).

• Build your horse's confidence gradually by leading him out around short and then longer routes you will eventually want to ride. Then progress to long-lining, where he will be operating more 'out on his own' (see pages 118–121), and finally riding.

• Plan a longer ride and transport your horse home in a trailer or lorry, so that he does not always anticipate and feel drawn towards the homeward stretch.

• If you have a trailer or lorry, transport your horse away from home to somewhere that is new to him, then ride him home. Without the draw of home (because he doesn't know where it is), he will most likely be happy to go wherever you ask and remain 'with' you, as he has nothing else on which to rely.

• Make sure your horse does not associate only home with the good things in life: friends, food, rest (see the box on page 180).

△ **Many horses have a problem with hacking 'alone', until you can convince them that in fact they are not – you are there too, and can be relied upon to take good decisions for both of you.**

Safety first

Whenever you are leading, long-lining or riding your horse on the roads, use high-visibility gear appropriate to the conditions. Traffic awareness and road safety considerations are paramount, especially if there is any chance of your horse suddenly stopping, rushing, spooking or shying.

Spooks and shies

Spooking is a horse's natural reaction when he spots an unusual object or sudden movement that might pose a threat. He needs to move quickly to get his head and body turned enough to focus on the danger clearly, and maybe put some distance between him and it. However, a horse will not naturally spook *a lot* as it uses up too much of his valuable energy, so if your horse does this when being ridden, it indicates that he feels the need constantly to look out for dangers, rather than being able to rely on you to take good decisions and keep you both safe.

It may also indicate that your horse is overfed and/or spends too much time confined in his stable, so the excess energy has to show up somewhere. If your horse suddenly begins spooking a lot when he has never been prone to it before, pain of some kind is often the cause.

• Check out your horse's lifestyle. If necessary, adjust his diet and/or give him more time out in the field (see Chapter 2). If appropriate, have him checked for possible causes of pain.

• Work on keeping your horse's attention with you, and yours with him, when hacking out. If you are in a dream yourself – and this is our natural tendency when we are enjoying a pleasant ride in the countryside – you cannot then expect your horse to pay attention to you at a moment's notice when he sees something scary. Keep taking the decisions and giving your horse instructions to follow: proactive riding will help to concentrate his mind on the job in hand rather than on what is going on around him.

• At home, work diligently on softness. A horse that is soft and relaxed with his head down will be less likely to spend his hacking time looking for dangers than one that is tight and tense and has his head in the air. He will also be easy to bring back to you instantly with a feel on the reins should the need arise.

• Also work on making your horse brave around scary objects (see pages 125–129). In particular, make sure he can cope calmly if a potentially frightening object, animal or vehicle appears suddenly, as these are relatively common occurrences when riding out.

△ **Riding along chatting to your friend and paying no attention to your horse may be fine by him – until it isn't. Always keep a good part of your focus on him, so that you are aware of how he is feeling and if necessary can step in to help him before he takes matters into his own hands.**

Baulks at unusual objects or hazards

This is another natural reaction from the horse: he does not believe it is safe to walk past that dustbin, step into that stream or go anywhere near that flock of sheep, so he simply stops and refuses to move. How you handle this situation can either help your horse overcome his fear and build his confidence in your judgement, or exacerbate the problem to where a simple stop becomes habitual or escalates into something worse.

• Check that you are the one taking the decisions in all other situations with your horse. If not, work on this aspect. He is then more likely to respond positively when you ask him to tackle something that worries him.

• Work at home on making your horse brave (see pages 123–127). Eventually, your horse will trust that whenever you ask him to do something, it will work out fine, even if initially he doesn't think he can cope.

• Make sure that when your horse does offer a step in the right direction, you remove all pressure (see box opposite).

• If your horse is really worried by something you have encountered, it is fine to get off and lead him. You are not 'giving in' or 'letting him win' – you are actually helping him gain in confidence – and it is also counterproductive to turn the situation into a huge issue. If possible, lead him backwards and forwards past or through the hazard several times, until he is completely relaxed about it, then remount and do the same from on top.

△ **Get your horse used to coping with hazards at home, before venturing out – just imagine if this were happening on a road full of traffic.**

△ **The horse is looking at the scary windmill (note his left ear) but sticking to the line the rider has set for him. This is what you want when you are out and about.**

△ **These well-prepared horses hack out calmly through woods and open spaces, where they are just as likely to meet wild deer or feral ponies as walkers, cyclists or an ice cream van.**

△ **On a hot day, the same pair are more than happy to cool off in a large pond en route.**

Goes slow away from home, rushes on the way back

The most likely cause here is again lack of confidence, so that the horse is reluctant to leave the safety of his familiar surroundings and then speeds home to be with his friends.

• Check first that your horse is not in pain or being restricted in his movement by an ill-fitting saddle. This will make him reluctant to move out freely, but on the way home adrenalin takes over and cancels out the discomfort.

• Check that your horse *really* understands the cue to move forward: he should respond promptly to just *one* use of the cue, *every* time. Also make sure it is you who decides the speed at all times. If not, work on these aspects at home (see pages 157–161).

• Transport your horse away from home to somewhere that is new to him, then ride him home. Without the draw of home (because he doesn't know where it is), you are more likely to be successful at regulating his speed at all times.

Remember to release

When dealing with situations where your horse gets 'stuck', good timing is crucial and is easily overlooked in the heat of the moment. It is essential that when he does offer to move forward from your cue, you release all pressure and simply go with his movement, even if he stops again almost straight away. Then ask again until he responds. Eventually, he will decide that moving forward is his best option.

If you continue to reapply your cue while your horse is moving in an effort to 'keep him going', in effect you are punishing him for the correct response, and he will have every reason to ignore your request and refuse to go any further. Make sure, too, that you are not blocking his forward movement by holding on to the reins or tensing your body and legs.

△ **This rider has worked hard with her mare over an extended period, both on the ground and in the saddle, to transform her from an anxious, erratic performer into a reliable pleasure horse. Here the mare canters in open fields at the speed the rider decides, on a slack rein.**

• Make sure your horse does not associate only home with the good things in life: friends, food, rest (see box below).

Dangerous problems

This category includes such things as rearing, bolting and bucking. There are many possible causes of these behaviours, but in each case the horse had probably already tried to show the rider in smaller ways that he was in difficulties. For example:
• A rider doesn't notice their horse's hesitation and reluctance the first few times they ask him to move forward while inadvertently keeping a strong contact on his mouth.
• The rider misreads the horse's confusion as laziness or napping, and punishes him for it with heavy leg cues and smacks with the stick. The horse then tries turning and moving backwards as possible answers to his dilemma, but both are met with the same tactics from the rider, who is becoming a little fearful and so hangs on to the reins even more tightly.
• When the horse cannot figure out what the rider wants, he panics under so much pressure and decides the only way out is to rear; the rider immediately loosens the reins, unintentionally rewarding the horse.

▽ **This little 'hop' may not look like much, and the rider is in no danger of falling off, but she should nevertheless take it seriously as a sign that the horse is experiencing difficulties. If she does not address it at this stage, the problem may manifest itself in more dangerous ways later on.**

- The rider decides to restrict the freedom of the horse's head and neck with a tight noseband and martingale, making it even more difficult for him to move forward.
- A number of repetitions later, the horse begins to offer rearing – almost to the vertical – as his first response to a request to move forward. The rider has had enough, dismounts and takes the horse back to his stable and friends – which constitutes a huge reward for his behaviour.

For safety's sake, with a horse that has developed such dangerous habits you need to get expert help. Even when you understand that the horse's problems are not of his own making, and believe he deserves all the help you can give him, it is essential that you also get real:
- Have the horse's behaviour patterns become too ingrained to be changed without exposing yourself and others to excessive physical danger?
- Practically, do you really have the time and money to expend on such an open-ended project, when you might be putting the effort into a horse that has not totally lost faith in people?
- Would it be fairer on the horse not to embark on his rehabilitation if you might have to give up halfway through?

As in everything you do with horses, the decisions are yours.

▽ **Rearing puts both horse and rider in an extremely precarious position. Retraining a horse that has developed it as his habitual response to stressful situations is a job for an expert.**

COMPETING

It is worth remembering that competition was invented by people, not horses! A horse can enjoy taking part, but if he has never competed he won't miss it – and in most horses' eyes it comes a poor second to hanging out in the field with their herd mates in any case. So, don't be pressured by others into competing with your horse on the basis that 'it's such as waste' just to have fun developing your relationship and hacking happily around the countryside together.

On the other hand, in an age where in most parts of the world horses no long have 'real jobs' to do, competition can give both you and your horse focus and purpose, and provide a positive motivation for you to work on improving your relationship and performance. The danger is that in your drive to be successful you may be tempted to sacrifice the horse's mental and/or physical well-being, whether momentarily in the heat of competition or long term.

To avoid this pitfall (to which many of us are prone), try to take a long-term view and use competition primarily to monitor your horse's progress. For your horse to remain calm and confident, compete at a level he already finds easy at home – it is unrealistic and unfair to expect him to cope well with the stresses of the competition atmosphere if he is also unprepared for the demands of the class.

Throughout this book I have talked about keeping your horse attentive, calm and soft in everything you do together. If you also make this – rather than winning, or even fulfilling the requirements of the class! – your primary focus in competition, the performance you want will inevitably follow – if not today, then tomorrow, or next week, or next month.

△ **Rounding up sheep on the moorland farm where she lives provides this mare with variety and purpose in her work, which also includes training in the arena and long rides out.**

△ **This rider has trained her horse for eventing with softness as her primary aim. As a result, she is able to take him safely cross-country in a simple snaffle and they are both thoroughly enjoying the experience.**

CONCLUSION

This book offers plenty for anyone involved in keeping and riding horses to think about. Some of the concepts and ideas may challenge knowledge you already have, others will simply confirm what you have always thought. The proof of any approach is, of course, does it work? Fortunately, your horse will always give you an honest answer.

When you start to look at horse-keeping, training and riding from the horse's point of view, you will find that even if the adjustments you make are small they can result in big changes in your horse. If you are new to these ideas, implement them gradually, take note of your horse's feedback, and make sure both of you are comfortable with how things are going before you move on. This way, you can ensure you both make steady progress and stay safe as you go.

Whatever you want to do with your horse, if you can see things from his perspective you will enable him to give of his best. Provide him with a lifestyle that suits his natural instincts, work to help him understand his training at every step of the way, and you will be rewarded with a horse that may yet fulfil all your dreams and ambitions. Riding should be fun for both of you, so stay positive – and above all, enjoy your horse.

ACKNOWLEDGEMENTS

The author and publishers would like to extend their grateful thanks to Margaret Linington-Payne, BHS Director of Standards, for her guidance and support, and also her team, Sam and Jenni, in the Training Department at the BHS. Thanks too to Jan Gigli of the BHS Merchandising Department for her encouragement and feedback over the years.

The photography for the book would not have been possible without a great number of people giving their time and expertise. All were gracious, patient and enthusiastic, even when asked to demonstrate 'getting it wrong' for the sake of the pictures! So huge thanks to all those who contributed to the photography, especially the riders and models: Amanda Barton, Marion Watt, Lynn Chapman, Carina Kane, Dianne Banks, Louise Banks, Angela Burgess and Lara Hoddinott. Thanks also to Lynn and Chris Chapman for their warm hospitality at Hazeley Farm House, and Debbie Saunders for kindly hosting us at Ladycross Lodge.

Useful Information

For further information about The British Horse Society and its work, including how to join, finding a BHS-qualified instructor or approved livery yard, access, welfare and safety, or Riding Club membership please go to www.bhs.org.uk, call +44 (0)8701 202244 or write to The British Horse Society, Stoneleigh Deer Park, Kenilworth, Warwickshire CV8 2XZ.

Tom & Sarah Widdicombe can be contacted about riding clinics via their website at www.bewithyourhorse.co.uk.

Lynn Chapman provides training and livery for horses and B&B for humans. She can be contacted via www.trainequus.co.uk.

Debbie Saunders is the Stable Manager at Ladycross Lodge, which offers both human and horse accommodation. Information is available at www.newforestholidays.uk.com.

Amanda Barton organises several clinics each year for trainers including Mark Rashid and Kathleen Lindley whose methods have been an inspiration in the creation of this book. Amanda can be reached via her website at www.amandabarton.co.uk.

For those interested in competing, information about FEI guidelines and definitions can be found at www.horsesport.org, the official website of the Fédération Equestre Internationale.

Readers in the USA may wish to contact the United States Equestrian Federation at 4047 Iron Works Parkway, 40511-8483 Lexington, USA, or on (1 859) 258 24 72 or visit their website at www.usef.org.

INDEX